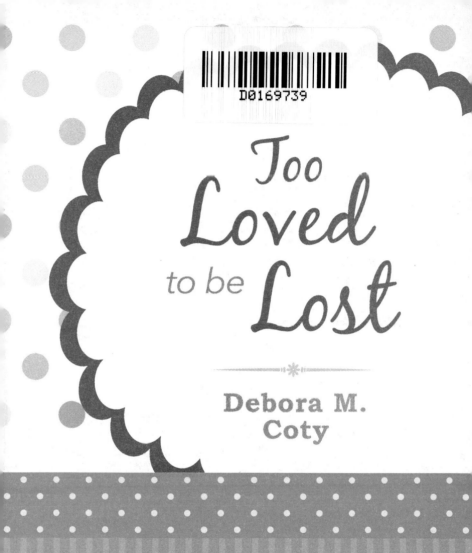

D0169739

Too
Loved
to be Lost

Debora M. Coty

SHILOH RUN PRESS
An Imprint of Barbour Publishing, Inc.

Print ISBN 978-1-62836-969-4

eBook Editions:
Adobe Digital Edition (.epub) 978-1-63058-634-8
Kindle and MobiPocket Edition (.prc) 978-1-63058-635-5

Published in association with the literary agency of WordServe Literary Group, Ltd., www.wordserveliterary.com.

Published by Shiloh Run Press, an imprint of Barbour Publishing, Inc., P.O. Box 719, Uhrichsville, Ohio 44683, www.shilohrunpress.com

Our mission is to publish and distribute inspirational products offering exceptional value and biblical encouragement to the masses.

Member of the
Evangelical Christian
Publishers Association

Printed in the United States of America.

Dedication

To my dear friend, Nancy Elizabeth Allen, whose
longtime loyalty and faithfulness epitomized
unconditional love gift-wrapped in a warm hug.
I miss you so, so much, girlfriend.

And to Chuck, my best friend, laughing buddy,
scripture go-to guy, techie extraordinaire, good-
sport-when-I-write-embarassing-things-about-
you, terrific dad and Pop-Pop, tolerator of
wifely quirks, chocolate stash provider, and long-
suffering spouse of 36 years. You've mirrored
Papa God's unconditional love for me in a
hundred different ways and it's the delight of my
life to grow weird with you.

Acknowledgments

❀ Big bear hugs to the wonderful folks at Barbour Publishing and my lovely longtime editor, Kelly McIntosh. You're the best!

❀ Eternal gratitude to WordServe Literary Agency and the audacious Greg Johnson.

❀ Special thanks to all the gracious people who shared their stories of Papa God's limitless love through the tough and triumphant times in their lives to encourage and uplift others: Sheila Iles; Rick Christensen; Tricia Pimental; Jimmy Crosby; Cheryl Bodden; Esther Hardy; Marianne Cali; Frances Swartz; Randy Martin; Caryl Music; Lynn, Sara, Cindy, Jan, Gloria, Jim, Carol Ettensohn; and Julie Cashin.

❀ More love than I can put into words to my wonderful family for always being there for me.

❀ Special hugs and pit sugar to my terrific three-year-old grandbuddy, Blaine, for reminding Mimi how utterly amazing unconditional love is.

❀ Above all, my deepest gratitude and praise goes to Papa God, the creator and source of hope, endurance, and everlasting love.

Contents

———— ❋ ————

Section 3: Woohoo! Road Trip!

Section 4: The Destination Is My Journey

Introduction

During my travels as a speaker, I've met lots and lots of women who view God as a stern, judgmental, impersonal entity lurking nearby with a huge frown and a big stick, just waiting to smite them to smithereens when they mess up. That perspective is usually based on harsh experiences they've had with an angry father, relentless coach, or strict teacher.

But you know what, girlfriend? That is so not Papa God.

Sure, our heavenly Father is holy and just. He's righteous and wants us to be, too. But that doesn't make Him a mean ol' hulking principal hovering in the hall with a big paddle.

Papa God has many other attributes as well—He's sovereign, ever present, kind, slow to anger, merciful, faithful, omniscient, and loving (to name a few). Did you know there are over fifty verses in the Bible describing our Creator's incredibly vast love for us? Listen, if assuring us of His unfailing love is that important to Him, it seems to me that we need to be picking up what He's putting down.

I'm often asked why I refer to Him as "Papa God." The reason is simple: because He is. My Papa. Your Papa. When we make the decision to believe in Him, to receive the unconditional love demonstrated by the sacrifice of His only Son, Jesus, in our place, we're adopted into Papa's family.[1] We become His beloved, adored, cherished daughters. Hey, we might not think we're much, but He thinks we're to die for!

The intimate term in the Bible for God the Father is the Aramaic word Abba, the name Jesus referred to Him by and offered to share with us as Papa's adopted children.[2] Children specifically chosen. Handpicked. Wanted. The Message translates "Abba" as

"Papa." I totally love that. It's warm, protective, and delightfully cuddly. What name could more richly express our close relationship with our heavenly Daddy?

That's what this book is all about—nurturing a closer relationship with Papa God. Getting on a heart level with the One who sees us through eyes of affection, not criticism. The One who isn't fixated on a list of dos and don'ts, but with the condition of our hearts. With Him it's not about what we do, it's about who we are through His lens of love.

And oh, does He ever love you and me. Intentionally. Unconditionally. Without limits.

I'm so happy you can join me in seeking a new herspective about love (my term for women seeing things in a fresh way). We'll explore life-enriching topics like learning to feel cherished, recognizing everyday miracles, developing trust, gaining confidence, overcoming depression, curbing anxiety, and healing hidden hurts. We'll find out how to survive collisions with difficult people and draw strength from our besties.

Above all, sister, won't you take my hand and spend time in Papa God's presence? The presence of the One who wants to lavish love on you.[3] (Really, how many people can you say that about?) The One who doesn't condemn or critique you but instead forgives and accepts you, quirks, meltdowns, zits, and all.

The One who, despite your imperfections, considers you His precious, precious daughter.

Yep. Spend some time with Him. Just see if you don't fall madly in love with your heavenly Papa, who already madly loves you. And always will.

Where Am I Going?
Can I Get There from Here?

*Praise the LORD! He is good.
God's love never fails.*
PSALM 136:1 CEV

CHAPTER 1

I Once Was Lost and Now I'm. . .Still Lost
(Gotta Start Somewhere)

Do not despise these small beginnings,
for the Lord rejoices to see the work begin.
ZECHARIAH 4:10 NLT

Our bus arrived in Edinburgh on Sunday around noon on a breezy, sunny, altogether gorgeous autumn day, and I was up for adventure. Scotland was the third country on the long-awaited UK tour Chuck and I had been enjoying in honor of our thirty-third wedding anniversary, and we were thrilled to be presented with a few free afternoon hours before a scheduled Scottish castle dinner at six o'clock. (Yep, I said *castle*! Woohoo! Bring on the glass slippers and flowing ball gown. . . . Cinderella, here I come!)

Chuck wanted to hit the sack for a catch-up nap after seven days of nonstop activity with our tour bus companions, but I was keen on exploring the ancient city. After all, our Scottish guide had said our hotel was only "a brisk walk" from bustling downtown Edinburgh.

I didn't want to waste a single minute. So after a brief check-in, I tossed my things into the hotel room and without more than a "See ya, honey!" I set off in the general direction in which the hotel clerk pointed.

Ah, the wonder of it all! I walked many miles, enjoying the

sights and sounds of the enchanting, romantic place, marveling at the intriguing architecture, the lovely Scottish accents, the cozy little coffee shop where J. K. Rowling painstakingly birthed Harry Potter, and the charming, heartwarming statue of Greyfriar's Bobby, the loyal little dog from the 1800s who'd sat on the grave of his beloved master in Greyfriar's Abbey cemetery every single day for fourteen years until his own death. The congregation of Greyfriar's fed Bobby and tried to lure him to shelter during the frigid winters, but he'd steadfastly refused to leave his master's grave.

Up to that point in my self-made tour, I had been keeping careful tabs of where I was in relation to where I'd been (Gaelic street signs, when they exist at all, are not very helpful). But I had been so deep in thought about dear Bobby that I turned a corner or two unawares.

Uh-oh. Where was I? It was then I realized that I'd left my cell phone back at the hotel. I had come away completely unprepared: no phone, no hotel name or address (we'd had a last-minute hotel substitution, which I hadn't written down), and a lousy sense of direction. The emergency number for our tour guide (whose first name was all I knew) was safe in Chuck's phone back at the hotel, which he'd turned off because of killer overseas roaming charges.

I didn't know what to do. I was embarrassed at my airheadedness. I couldn't even ask a policeman for help; I didn't know where I was staying or who to look for.

So I just kept walking. Walking and praying that at any moment I'd see something familiar that would give me a clue which direction to go. I hoofed it for nearly three hours, alone and lost in a bustling city, growing more frantic by the moment. I knew if I didn't find my way soon, I'd be kissing my dreamy castle dinner farewell. It seemed as though I was walking in gigantic circles. Sure enough, by the third time I encountered wee Bobby's statue,

I knew I was in trouble.

As I stood there staring at Bobby, internally wailing to Papa God in desperation and about to collapse to the curb in tears, I heard a woman's voice call out on the crowded street, "Hat girl! Oh, hat girl!"

Me? Could she mean me?

I touched the brim of my adorable black-and-gray tweed newsman's cap (one of four hats I'd purchased already on the trip—I *am* a hat girl, you know) and turned to find the smiling faces of a couple from our tour group who just happened to be passing by. With a map. And the name of our hotel.

In the midst of thousands of tourists traipsing the busy streets of the sprawling city, they'd somehow spotted me. They didn't know my name but recognized me because of the hats I'd worn every day on the bus.

Despite my fatigue and blistered feet, I had to laugh. My heavenly Papa had used my hat fetish—a weird personal habit of mine, which He knew as well as He knows all your silly personal quirks—to bail me out of a disaster of my own making. And it happened right in front of the statue of Bobby. . .a tribute to faithfulness.

Luck? Nah. Coincidence? No way. My Savior might as well have written across the sky with a giant black Sharpie, "I love you even when you screw up, dear child. You are precious to Me, quirks and all. Just like the extraordinary loyalty displayed by little Bobby here, I will *always* be faithful to you, even beyond death."

LOVE THAT JUST WON'T QUIT

And in a nutshell, that's what Papa God's unconditional love is: Forever faithfulness. Limitless loyalty. Enduring allegiance. Eternal devotion. Spiritual security.

Let's explore these marvelous qualities.

❀ Forever faithfulness: "He has never let you down, never looked the other way when you were being kicked around. He has never wandered off to do his own thing; he has been right there, listening" (Psalm 22:24 MSG). In other words, whether you realized it or not, Papa was there during those times when you felt discouraged or miserable or hopeless. (Even when you were lost and alone in a foreign city!) He was still right by your side, faithfully preparing His next move to help you find your way.

❀ Limitless loyalty: His love for us won't fit in a box. There are no confining sides, top, or bottom. No conditions, qualifications, or rules that we must abide by or we're out. No barriers, not even when our present earth suits expire. "Neither death nor life. . .nor height nor depth. . .shall be able to separate us from the love of God which is in Christ Jesus our Lord" (Romans 8:38–39 NKJV).

❀ Enduring allegiance: You pledge allegiance to the flag, your country, your club, sometimes your job. In your marriage vows you pledge allegiance to your spouse. But get this: Papa God pledges allegiance to you. To *you*. To the good and bad, the inconsistent and obsessive, the sensible and crazy all rolled up into the bundle that is you. And He vows that nothing you could ever do or think or say will drive Him away. *Nothing.* "Never will I leave you; never will I forsake you" (Hebrews 13:5 NIV). How utterly amazing is that?

❀ Eternal devotion: When you were a little girl, didn't you dream of Prince Charming galloping up on a white charger and sweeping you off your feet to live happily ever after? Maybe you still dream that. (Maybe I've been thinking about castles entirely too much lately.) But you grew up and realized that fairy tale is unrealistic when it comes to flesh-and-blood lovers. . . . *Happily ever after* is awfully hard to come by if you're dependent on a fallible man to supply all the elements that make you happy. Imperfect human relationships might be ever after; however, they're certainly not 100 percent happy. But you know what? It's not a fairy tale when it comes to the Lover of your soul. It's reality. He adores you. He perceives nothing but the very best in you and thinks you're the most beautiful thing He's ever seen. He loves you with a passionate romance that will never, *ever* end.

❀ Spiritual security: I once raised a baby squirrel that my cat helped fall out of the nest. When I wasn't feeding him with an eyedropper, that tiny, hairless, helpless creature loved to curl up in my warm, safe pocket and go wherever I went. He could rest in complete security there, free from anxiety or harm, knowing I was watching over him. That's what spiritual security is for us, too—feeling that we're snug and safe, curled up in the pocket of Jesus' jeans. "In God I trust and am not afraid. What can man do to me?" (Psalm 56:11 NIV). Regardless of what happens to our earth costumes—and one day, inevitably, the temporary bodies we currently live in will fade away—our security is in knowing that our spirits, our true selves, will live on forever with the One who loves us more than anyone on earth ever could.

Like the parable Jesus told about the lost sheep (meaning us!) in the fifteenth chapter of Luke (read verses 1–6 to refresh your memory), we can never stray from our Shepherd to the point of no return. He loves us far too much to let us go. I find that marvelously reassuring, don't you?

So when you lose your way and begin to wander, whether it's spiritually, emotionally, mentally, or physically (hey, I can get lost in a tote bag), be assured that Papa will find you. Know why? Because you, sister, are too loved to be lost.

DINNER, SHREK STYLE

By the way, despite my lengthy detour, I did make it to the Scottish castle dinner. Unfortunately, the food wasn't as magically fairy tale–ish as the medieval ambiance. They served "neeps and tatties" (turnips and potatoes) alongside "haggis," a traditional Scottish savory pudding containing—are you sitting down?—sheep's heart, liver, and lungs, encased in the sheep's stomach. It wobbled like a fat, black, gooey sausage.

Gulp.

Anyone need a slightly stained ball gown?

To succeed in life, you need three things:
a wishbone, a backbone, and a funnybone.
~REBA McENTIRE

FOLLOWING MY PERSONAL GPS (GOD-POWERED SATELLITE)

1. Can you recall a time when you felt hopelessly lost? How were you finally found?

2. Is there someone in your life who has demonstrated extraordinary faithfulness to you? How? Did you in turn feel faithful to him or her?

3. Are there people who have let you down because their loyalty was limited? How did their betrayal affect you?

4. Would you say that you feel assured of spiritual security? Why or why not?

5. One last smidgeon of advice from someone who truly understands wandering in physical, emotional, and spiritual circles: When you're feeling lost, forget faux pride. Stop, roll down your window, and ask for directions from the one holding the map.

CHAPTER 2

Singed by the Dragon
(Overcoming Burnout)

———※———

Are you tired? Worn out?
Burned out? . . . Come to me.
MATTHEW 11:28 MSG

Oh. My. Merciful. Heavens. What on earth was happening?

My husband, twenty-eight-year-old daughter, two-year-old grandson, and I had no clue when we found ourselves—in our SUV with a luggage topper—suddenly surrounded by more than a hundred roaring motorcycles racing at breakneck speed around crazy-steep curves as we traversed the Appalachians to visit friends in Tennessee. They swarmed us like gigantic, angry, black leather–jacketed bees, their frightening collective buzz nearly deafening.

Although there was no good place to pull off the twisting mountain road, we wedged the car sort of half-on and half-off to make way for the incredible black swarm that just kept coming. Motorcycle after motorcycle zipped by us, each nearly horizontal, their handlebars inches from the asphalt as they flew around the sharp curves. I saw sparks fly more than once as metal scraped pavement, and I just knew we'd round the next curve to find a motorcycle wrapped around a tree and body parts strewn everywhere.

We soon learned that we'd inadvertently wandered onto the Tail of the Dragon,[4] "America's most twisted beast." This jagged strip of US-129 on the border of North Carolina and Tennessee boasts 318 curves in eleven miles and has claimed more than twenty lives since 2000 (and no doubt more before someone started keeping score). With no houses or intersecting roads to impede the flow, speed junkies from all over the world descend on the Dragon to try their skill on death-defying twists such as "Beginners End," a hairpin turn called "The Whip," and a fly-off-the-handle hump known as "Gravity Cavity."

So there we were, a misplaced, seat-belted, all-about-safety family, just trying to stay on the road as we zigged through all these horrific zags, praying madly, wide-eyed and green around the gills as the adults downed Bonine and the baby lost his breakfast repeatedly until he was limp as a dishrag.

When we finally nosed our car into the parking lot of the Dragon's one and only gas station, I was stunned to see a make-shift memorial to the scores of people who had fallen to the Dragon by injury or death. A huge pile of broken, twisted metal from demolished motorcycles and wrecked cars formed a towering macabre sculpture testifying to the horrible possibilities of your own fate if you chose to continue on this road.

Yet they kept on coming.

We just don't think it could ever happen to us, do we?

Yep, us. You and me. We may not be motorcycle mamas (do ATVs count?), but I'm not talking about straddling Harleys here. There's another dragon that claims our lives piece by piece. . .joyful moment by joyful moment. . .one irreplaceable sliver of vitality at a time, until it whittles away our motivation for going on and wrecks our inner peace. It's called burnout. This fiery dragon breathes stress that just won't end—relentless weariness that evolves into depression, hopelessness, and a wrecked life.

You know exactly what I'm talking about, don't you? This

dragon has whacked you right off your feet with his wickedly spiked tail a time or two.

But sister, we don't want to become twisted, macabre memorials to the burnout dragon—broken pieces of our lives piled high in testimony of our inability to handle ridiculous schedules, unstable health, rocky marriages, troubled relationships, or choking finances. We must somehow learn how to defeat our personal dragon and choose to *not* stay on the same road that has brought us this far on the route to disaster.

THAT'S GRATITUDE FOR YA

My friend Sheila is well acquainted with the burnout dragon. Besides working twelve-hour shifts, she takes care of her mother, who suffers with dementia, and her ninety-two-year-old stepfather. Some days the stress and fatigue seem overwhelming, and Sheila feels resentful of having to forfeit her days off to do their grocery shopping, cooking, house cleaning, and laundry. She admits to wondering more than once, "Is my life on hold until they pass away?"

On one such day, after picking up her mom and stepdad's groceries, Sheila was en route to their home to take care of these thankless chores, working up a major attitude. It just wasn't fair. Why should she have to give up so much of her limited time and energy to help people who didn't really appreciate it?

When she entered the house and began unpacking groceries, Sheila wasn't particularly surprised when her mom wandered into the kitchen and began crying. She did that sometimes when she felt "lost." But she was far from lost that day. Through warm, grateful tears, Sheila's mother thanked the Lord aloud for her daughter, for the groceries she brought, and for all she did for them.

As Sheila recalls, "My selfish attitude flew right out the window. Those hugs and snippets of appreciation were priceless. My exhaustion suddenly lifted. I no longer felt resentful and went on to spend five hours doing laundry and cleaning with a different heart—a cheerful heart—and a smile on my face."

As she heard her mother singing happily in the background while she worked, Sheila realized that Papa God had seen her granite-hard heart prior to her arrival and knew she needed a heart transplant. "I will give you a new heart and put a new spirit within you; I will take the heart of stone out of your flesh and give you a heart of flesh" (Ezekiel 36:26 NKJV).

HEY, I CAN BLOW FIRE OUT OF MY NOSTRILS, TOO

Sheila's story demonstrates some effective dragon-slaying tools that can help us all defend ourselves against burnout. I'm also including some updated tips from my book, *Too Blessed to Be Stressed.*

Remember that you're truly appreciated.

You may not ever receive sufficient thanks from others for all you do, but when you feel bummed over it, remind yourself that Papa God sees every little detail and is well aware of the sacrifices and effort you extend to serve others in your family, job, church, community. . .the inhabitants of your little world. Papa sees it all—every dollar you spend, all the time and energy you put in, each hour of sleep you miss, all the things you give up for someone else's benefit—and He truly appreciates *you* acting as His fingers and toes on earth.

One day He'll reward you with the immense gratitude you deserve, but brace yourself, it may not be till heaven. In the meantime, lean not on fallible people but on Papa as your source of validation and satisfaction for a job well done and a life well lived.

Give your constipated calendar an activities enema.

Determine your top three priorities—the ministries Papa has assigned to you at this particular season of your life (and yes, your family definitely counts as a ministry!). Write those three priorities (*only* three for simplicity's sake) on an index card. Sit down with your calendar and card; study next month's constipated daily schedule. Bathe it in prayer. Then ruthlessly slash everything not conducive to your three priorities. Time to flush the excess.

Grab your phone (do it now while your motivation's hot) and explain to the Grand Poobah responsible for each deleted activity that you're simplifying, scaling back, washing away everything unrelated to the specific ministries the Lord has assigned to you. These are what you need to focus your finite time and energies on.

Stand firm in your resolve, and don't be swayed by guilt. You and I both know some folks have the guilt-you gift, but this is the time to woman up and repeat as many times as necessary: "Sorry, but no. Sorry, but no." Got that? You hereby have permission to say *no*. And memorize this verse: "Our purpose is to please God, not people" (1 Thessalonians 2:4 NLT).

❀ Remeber that you're truly apprciated.

❀ Give your constipated calendar an activities enema.

❀ Simplify, yes, but preserve the important stuff.

❀ Tape those three priorities to your mirror where you'll see them every day. Schedule time with the peeps who matter most: your husband, your children, and *you*, girl.

❀ Get physical. Especially after spending hours on the computer.

❈ Avoid CCCB (Computer Chair Cauliflower Buns) and relax knotted shoulder muscles by simple stretching exercises I've compiled during my thirty-five years as a health-care professional in physical therapy clinics. You'll find these amid a dozen Two-Minute Stress Busters (videos designed for busy gals like you that only last, well . . .two minutes!) at my website, www.DeboraCoty.com.

❈ Look for Papa's fingerprints on your every day. I call them grace notes, proof that He's there, He's aware, and He cares.

❈ More about grace notes in chapter 9, but the point for now is that we're often so busy treading water in the stress-pool of living that we overlook the evidence that a strong hand is keeping us afloat. Nothing burns us out faster than thinking we're doing life on our own. We're not. But you'll see His life preserver surrounding you only if you open your spiritual eyes and look for it.

❈ Tap into a greater strength than your own.

❈ You and I both know that our meager strength is not enough. We can tell by the scuff marks on our bellies as we drag into bed at night. Thank heavens there's an industrial-strength stain stick that'll take care of those pesky scuff marks once and for all. "The joy of the LORD is your strength" (Nehemiah 8:10 NIV).

Sure enough, it's joy! Joy as in joy-filled, joyous, and joybulescence. Okay, maybe I made up that last one, but it's a great word picture of what our lives *could* be like if we sincerely ask to be filled with the joy of the Lord and commit to focus on that joy.

You know, joy is not a reaction, it's a transaction. A decision. A commitment. Not to be confused with happiness, which is dependent on our external circumstances, the joy of the Lord is a filling from within, having nothing to do with what happens to us. It's more about what's happening *through* us. Because it's supernatural, it really can't be explained, but genuine Jesus-joy provides wondrous strength to rise above the muck and mundane. I can personally attest that it's real. And powerful. And waiting to transform you into a world-class dragon slayer.

So what'll it be, girlfriend? Who will end up a casualty—you or your dragon? Will your legacy be a twisted pile of handlebars and headlights, broken hearts and busted dreams? Or will you raise your sword at the end of the road, proud, joyful, and triumphant?

David threw the stone, but Papa God threw the giant.
~DEBORA M. COTY

FOLLOWING MY PERSONAL GPS (GOD-POWERED SATELLITE)

1. Has the burnout dragon been breathing smoke down your neck? In what way?

2. We can get a lot of mileage out of a little gratitude, can't we? But sometimes thanks for all we do is hard to come by. How does Philippians 2:3 relate? "Do nothing from selfishness or empty conceit, but with humility of mind regard one another as more important than yourselves" (NASB).

3. Does your constipated calendar need an activity enema? Or at least a little de-clogging? Okay, let's get started. What are your top three priorities? Take a look at your schedule. How many things do you do that are unrelated to these priorities? What's your next move? (You do realize, don't you, that if *you* don't do anything about it, it'll never change?) C'mon, girl, don't end up in a scrap heap.

4. Stop right now and hop over to my website, www.DeboraCoty.com. Now hover over "Stress Busters" and choose a video. After you've enjoyed that one, click on number ten, "Protecting Our Earth Suits" and let 'er rip. Do the stretching exercises along with us. Believe me—once they become a habit, you'll have a sharp arrow in your quiver to fight the burnout dragon. I've seen them rock the world of my patients.

5. So how about inserting a little joybulescence into your life? The key to releasing yourself to joy is trusting that Papa God has your back. Can you think of a time when the joy of the Lord lightened your day? "I always see the Lord near me, and I will not be afraid with him at my right side. Because of this, my heart will be glad, my words will be joyful, and I will live in hope" (Acts 2:25–26 CEV).

CHAPTER 3

Gaining Perspective
(Seeing Things in a Whole New Way)

He has brought down rulers from
their thrones, but has lifted up the humble.
LUKE 1:52 NIV

I felt my face prickle with heat, but this time it wasn't a hot flash. It was the humiliating realization that I was a have-not in the presence of an elite gathering of haves. A nobody in a room full of somebodies. Although the dividing wall between us was transparent, it was quite real, and its ramifications were loud and clear: I was an outsider.

And woe was me. I was stuck with this lot for weeks to come.

I came home from that first encounter feeling wretched. I had been repeatedly stuffed onto the bottom shelf or worse, ignored completely. It was a severe blow to my self-worth. I realized I was going to have to find some way to endure the situation, because it wasn't going away.

It would feel like being chosen last for the eighth-grade kickball team every single week for the entire school year.

So I did the least and the most I could do. I prayed.

"Lord, please show me how to hold my own with these people. I know they're better and more experienced than me at this particular activity, and my best will never be good enough for them. So please help me endure. No, not just endure, but enjoy myself. . .if that's even possible."

Of course it's possible, dearest Debbie, my forlorn heart heard in reply. *I'm the lifter of your head.*

Where had I heard that before? Ah, yes—the verse in my personal devo just the previous week (probably not a coincidence, huh?): "You, O LORD, are a shield about me, my glory, and the One who lifts my head" (Psalm 3:3 NASB).

After letting that scripture marinate a few hours, sure enough, I felt my chin begin to lift and my shoulders de-slump as I rose to my full five feet in height. My worth comes from my standing with Jesus, not my standing with mere humans.

I reasoned that none of us will be a have in every situation we find ourselves. There will always be someone more talented, wealthy, knowledgeable, beautiful, skinny, clever, boobalicious. . .*whatever.* Who cares? I don't need to win. Keep the sash and tiara.

So I decided to quit being a humiliated have-not and become a happy have-not.

INNIES VERSUS OUTIES

Oh, we all know they exist, the haves and the have-nots. The roster and pecking order changes in every setting—work, church, organizations, families, community events—but in every social circle in which we orbit, there seems to always be the innies and the outies.

The haves (innies) are the "accepted" clique in a specific environment. . .the players, the movers and shakers, the got-it-on girls, the cool chicks. They're quietly respected—the natural leaders others seem to automatically fall in line behind. Often they're the ones with the highest skill level or those who have achieved the most acclaim or accomplishments within the tribe. They aren't necessarily boastful or cocky; some are actually quite humble. But they definitely *belong*, and everyone knows it. It's a given.

Then there are the have-nots (outies). They're the ones who might hang out with the group members but somehow are not the same. They're on a different level—a slightly lower level—and although the haves may be overtly friendly enough and include them as part of the whole, there's an invisible barrier that separates them and they're never really *in* the group, only *with* the group.

Outies are well aware that they don't belong and are existing on the fringe; they never quite feel comfortable. Or safe.

Depending upon the setting, sometimes we're innies, sometimes we're outies. But whether the delicate outcasts happen to be us or someone else, we need to be cognizant that to varying degrees outies feel unloved. Unworthy. Uncared about.

LET'S CUDDLE

As self-respecting women, we should proactively avoid subjecting ourselves to that desperate have-not inadequacy that drains our confidence, makes us doubt our worth, and sabotages our self-esteem. It's best to follow the wisdom imparted by a plaque I once saw: "Go where you're celebrated, not where you're tolerated."

But we all know there are times when we have no choice. We're thrust into circumstances beyond our control and must somehow come to grips with that dreadful outie inferiority we feel whenever we're with certain people we can't escape. Times when we need more than anything to be understood, comforted, and well. . .cuddled.

So remember—when you're feeling unloved and unlovable, it's time to CUDDLE:

❀ C: Climb up into Papa God's lap. Just like when you were a little girl and yearned to feel big, warm arms wrap around you and a gentle, loving voice whisper everything will be okay. Press your head to His chest. Close your eyes. Feel Him stroke your back. Hear His heartbeat. Know that you are profoundly cherished.

❀ U: Unload. Drop that heavy load you carry—you know exactly what I mean. The one that drags you down and keeps you feeling perpetually bad about yourself. Often it's exacerbated by fatigue. Take a look at your schedule and consider a diagnosis of calendar constipation (described in chapter 2). Would you benefit from an activity enema? Trim. Hack. Simplify. Take control of your schedule before it controls you.

❀ D: Daydream. Refuse to answer your phone for a whole hour. Step away from your to-do list. Ignore your e-mail. Unplug emotionally. Allow the sweet sound of silence to bathe you in healing rose-scented water. Lie down somewhere—outdoors if at all possible. Take three deep breaths. Exhale. Now ask yourself a fun open-ended question such as, "Where would I go on vacation if I could go anywhere in the world?" or "If I were in a movie, who would I want as my costar?" and allow your imagination to run wild like those carefree childhood summer days long past. You have now opened up a window of happiness. Wait—don't shut it yet!

❀ D: Dance to the music deep in your soul. Turn the volume up on that soul song you usually keep muted. Fling out your arms, and boogie in a sunbeam. Get your bad self down in the cookie aisle. Laugh as you twirl in the rain. Dance until you drop. It's oh so much better than collapsing from stress-induced exhaustion.

❀ L: Let go of your imagined unworthiness. Listen to me, dear girl: Your worth is infinitely greater than the Hope Diamond. You are loved. You are important. You are cherished. No one can make you feel unloved without your permission. Reject rejection. Know this: Papa God will *never* reject you.

❀ E: Evolve into a higher being. When you climb down from Papa's lap refreshed, don't turn around and go right back to the same behaviors that sent you screaming into the night. You're not a dog returning to its vomit; you're a tenderly cuddled woman of God who is adored and beloved. Now act like it. Pull your shoulders back. Smile. Resolve to treat yourself like your own BFF. When others see how much you respect yourself, they'll respect you, too.

THIS GIRL'S GOT GAME

Healthy self-esteem is a primary ingredient to getting new her-spective (by the way, the female point of view is often quite different from hisspective!) and becoming a happy have-not. I met a woman who had a tremendous impact on me—a woman who might have easily considered herself a humiliated have-not but absolutely refused.

The moment I entered the county fair restroom, I knew it was different. Unlike the grody, grimy, get-your-business-over-quickly-and-flee-this-nasty-place fare I'd come to expect from public toilets, this one actually gleamed.

It had, in fact, a sort of ethereal feel to it, if you can imagine as much from such an unlikely place. There existed no black, icky grime in the corners, no stray sprinkles or puddles on the floor, no graffiti on the stall doors. Everything was shiny. A delightful whiff of gardenias scented the air, and someone with a very pleasant voice was cheerfully humming.

It was. . .well, *lovely.*

I momentarily forgot I was in the bowels of a county fair midway and thought, *Now this is the kind of place you'd like to kick back and stay for a while.*

Upon exiting my stall, I noticed two white-uniformed attendants busily polishing counters and sinks and realized one was the source of the lively humming that perked up the place. I couldn't help but comment about the surprising cleanliness of the bathroom. She straightened, held her head high, smiled from ear to ear, and said, "There's not a speck of dirt beneath, behind, or across our seats. You can go to any other bathroom in the whole park, and trust me, you'll come back here. We're the best!"

I left that bathroom completely uplifted from the obvious pride this woman took in her work and her contagiously glowing self-esteem that immediately transferred to me and made my respect for her soar.

I want to be like that, I decided right then and there. I want to change my herspective to be all about serving and uplifting others. I want to do my job so well that neither I nor anyone else will be deterred by any invisible barriers. And my job—regardless of why I'm there—is to reflect Papa God's all-accepting love.

Nobody wants to be around a pouty outie.

HERSPECTIVE THAT ROCKS

So did my new and improved attitude work? You betcha. And it still does. Turns out that my affiliation with the haves I mentioned earlier is going to be long-term (as in years rather than weeks), but it really hasn't been a problem since my herspective changed. Oh, I'm still not included in innie chic-chats or inside jokes, but it doesn't sting anymore. I've been surprised by how many new friends I've made when I've made the effort to reach out to individuals (mostly other outies but some innies, too) and take an interest in their personal lives. To make them feel cared about. To make sure they *belong*.

Uplifting one new person at each gathering has become my focus. My mantra: It's not about me. It's about us. Individual rings linked together become a strong, beautiful chain, each segment an integral part. Each important. Each esteemed.

How about you? Is there a musty corner of your life in which you feel like an outsider? Could it be time to CUDDLE, change your herspective, and become a happy have-not?

Take my advice, girlfriend—when someone looks down at you, fix your gaze over his or her shoulder on the smiling face of Jesus.

The final beatitude should be: Blessed
are the flexible for they shall not break.

~DEB DEARMOND

FOLLOWING MY PERSONAL GPS (GOD-POWERED SATELLITE)

1. Think of one group you're a part of in which you feel quite comfortable and safe. . .like you belong. Now list three things that make you a have (innie) with those particular people. No guilt here, girlfriend; there's nothing wrong with being on the inside track.

2. What can you do to become more aware of the outies in that group? How can you make them feel more accepted and less like a humiliated have-not?

3. Now consider one affiliation with which you feel like a have-not (an outie). Can you think of three reasons why you're an outsider with this group? Are there other have-nots there? Have you ever tried linking with them?

4. Okay, 'fess up: Are you a pouty outie? What can you do to change your herspective and become a happy have-not?

5. Have you enjoyed a good CUDDLE with Papa God lately? Review the acronym, and schedule yourself CUDDLE time during the upcoming week. Seriously, you'll be so glad you did, and afterward you'll be able to say, like David, "I feel put back together" (PSALM 18:23 MSG).

CHAPTER 4

Topping off My Tank
(Strength for the Journey)

You were tired out by the length of your road,
yet you did not say, "It is hopeless."
You found renewed strength,
therefore you did not faint.

ISAIAH 57:10 NASB

||||||||||||||||||||||||||||||||||||||||||||||||||||||||||||||||||||||||||||||||||||||||||||||||||||||||||||||||||||||||||||||

Not long ago, a dear writer chum and strong Christ-follower, Rick, happily volunteered to *walk with* my niece, Andie, an aspiring writer, at the annual Florida Inspirational Writers Retreat, which I codirect.

My niece is an awesome girl; actually, I should say woman, since she's now a junior at the University of South Florida majoring in English (with an A average, I might proudly add!). But Andie has some lifelong physical disabilities due to cerebral palsy that make it difficult for her to get around. Especially stairs like the two flights we had to climb to get to the lunch hall and then back down to the meeting rooms with no elevator available.

And her eyesight is extremely limited, so she needs assistance finding her way around anywhere new and sorting out written instructions and correspondence, such as the myriad of handouts we encountered at the retreat.

Knowing that I would be tied up running the show (my codirector was ill), Rick graciously volunteered to be Andie's buddy for the retreat, meeting her at the door when she arrived and *walking with* her throughout the day. He never rushed her, never made her feel that she was dragging him down. He made sure she got everything done and everywhere she needed to be, all the while bantering amiably and putting her at ease in what could have been a trying situation. Thanks to Rick, Andie thoroughly enjoyed herself.

Now there's something else about Rick you should know. He also voluntarily *walks with* his widowed sister-in-law during her battle against cancer on the opposite coast of Florida. That means on many weekends after a long workweek, he detours off his own path, forfeiting free time with his family and special interests (besides being a devotional writer, Rick's a superb amateur photographer) to travel across the state to simply be with his sister-in-law and support her in her wellness journey.

By Rick's example, I've learned that to *walk with* someone in this sense, the stronger partner subtly paces himself to the stride of the weaker. He makes no hoopla about it. He just quietly does it. Without being condescending in the least, he offers emotional support and gentle guidance, often by just being there, although at times he must actually physically support his friend.

By his presence, he shares his strength when she hasn't enough of her own.

He silently sacrifices his own comfort, desires, and needs to cover those of his companion. The weaker partner knows that he or she is being looked after and lovingly protected. Because she trusts him, she is then able to relax and lean into the reliable, caring encirclement of the stronger partner.

Much like Papa God *walks with* us.

His very presence gives us strength for our own journey.

But how, you ask, can we be assured of His mighty presence when we can't see Him with our proof-starved eyes? How can we access the power, the vigor, the potency of His strength when we need it most?

The answer I've found is simple, portable, and oh so sweet. Life Savers. Oh yeah, you read that right. Life Savers.

SWEET. TOTALLY.

Life Saver "flavor of month" scriptures are a toothsome idea I came up with to help me focus on a short, pithy, powerful new verse each month to stock my spiritual pantry. You know how when you get a midnight craving for death by chocolate cake, you come completely unglued if you don't have all the ingredients on hand in your kitchen pantry?

Well, this is a way you can keep your spiritual pantry chock-full of the necessary ingredients for living a Jesus-led life so that whenever you need them, you won't go away hungry.

Remember, God's Word equals God's strength. When you reach the end of your rope, you'll find Jesus there with a ladder. Or a parachute. "Be strong in the Lord and in his mighty power" (Ephesians 6:10 NLT). But when problems pop up, we don't always have our Bibles, computers, or i-devices handy to access that appropriate-to-the-immediate-circumstance verse we just can't seem to put our thumbs on.

So the best place to store God's Word is in your personal hard drive. Your brain.

But you and I both know memorizing scripture can be a problem with our crazy-busy schedules and nonstop responsibilities. Who has the time or energy? No worries. Life Savers to the rescue!

When my sister and I were little girls squirming and whining in the church pew on Sunday mornings (those were pre–children's church days when five-year-olds began tormenting their parents—

and everyone else—in big church), my momma would pass down a roll of butter rum Life Savers to stifle us. It worked the same way music calms the savage beast. Better than chomping gum or unwrapping peppermint candies from noisy crinkly wrappers, Life Savers were the perfect quiet treat, socially acceptable for antsy kids in a worship service. Those little rings of goodness were sweet, engaging, and satisfying.

Fast-forward five decades and I'm still devouring Life Savers. And they're still sweet, engaging, and satisfying. Only now they're the Bread of Life instead of candy.

I share my Life Savers with lots of women at conferences and speaking events, and they dig this uncomplicated, user-friendly system for scripture memorization so much that I'd like to share it with you, too. More than just butter rum, the variety of flavors will blow you away. (You know, the only trouble with candy Life Savers is that the flavors are not very adventuresome—why don't they come up with Smokin' Mocha, Chillin' Cheesecake, or Mind-Melting Fudgie Mint Ripple?)

Okay, here's how it works: Right now, this very minute before you get sidetracked, grab your calendar and record one Life Saver from the list beginning on page 42 beside the name of each month (doesn't matter whether you start in January or November; finish out the rest of this year and do it again on next year's calendar when the time comes). On the first day of the month, memo the Life Saver you've chosen for that month on your i-device and/ or jot it on sticky notes to post in all the places you'll be sure to notice—your bathroom mirror, your car's console, the Godiva stash in your underwear drawer. You know, your hot spots.

Then every time you run across your monthly Life Saver, repeat it aloud three times (the flavor comes through best when you wrap your tongue around it) and let it melt into your heart.

Consider the meaning of each word. Savor the Saver. Suck the joy out of that spiritual treat until it's completely digested and permanently implanted in your innards.

FILL 'ER UP AND WATCH 'ER GO

Talk about an infusion of strength! It's like topping off your gas tank. You're revved up and raring to go anywhere.

You'll be amazed by how many times Papa uses that very verse to speak *to* you and *through* you during that month. By the year's end, you'll have twelve new decision-impacting verses memorized! And best of all, they'll be imprinted in your gray matter hard drive for easy reference the rest of your life.

While traveling the narrow, twisting, mountainous roads of Italy's Amalfi Coast on our anniversary trip last fall, I drew great inspiration from four simple words someone had painted on the sheer white cliffs: "You'll never walk alone." Somehow I think I'll remember that plain but profound message long after my memories of the magnificent Sistine Chapel and statue of David fade.

Incidentally, there are different ways the Lord goes about walking with us, especially us stubborn gals. You know Mary Stevenson's marvelous poem, "Footprints in the Sand"? Well, here's the Debora Coty version: When I look back on the beach of my life, there are times I see Papa's footprints and mine side by side. Then there are times I see one set of prints; that, of course, was when He carried me. But then there are these weird trenches every few yards. That's when He dragged me by my feet.

As promised, here's my Life Saver list. There are twenty-four (two years' worth) short but sweet scriptures (all twenty words or less) that pack the biggest punch for me. Most are from The Message translation because that's the version I was reading when

I began collecting Life Savers (I read a different translation each year), but feel free to add more of your own. Papa's got hundreds of flavors to choose from!

LIFE SAVERS

❀ "God is greater than our worried hearts" (1 John 3:20 MSG).

❀ "Let your living spill over into thanksgiving" (Colossians 2:7 MSG).

❀ "Let's not sleepwalk through life like those others" (1 Thessalonians 5:6 MSG).

❀ "I sought the LORD, and He answered me, and delivered me from all my fears" (Psalm 34:4 NASB).

❀ "It's the praising life that honors me" (Psalm 50:23 MSG).

❀ "May the Master pour on the love so it fills your life and splashes over on everyone around you" (1 Thessalonians 3:12 MSG).

❀ "Kindness should begin at home" (1 Timothy 5:4 TLB).

❀ "The Day is coming when you'll have it all—life healed and whole" (1 Peter 1:5 MSG).

❀ "If we are faithless, he remains faithful" (2 Timothy 2:13 NIV).

❀ "Our God gives you everything you need, makes you everything you're to be" (2 Thessalonians 1:2 MSG).

❀ "Don't hit back; discover beauty in everyone"
   (Romans 12:17 MSG).

❀ "Live carefree before God; he is most careful with you"
   (1 Peter 5:7 MSG).

❀ "Encourage one another and build each other up"
   (1 Thessalonians 5:11 NIV).

❀ "I'm so grateful to Christ Jesus for making me adequate
   to do this work" (1 Timothy 1:12 MSG).

❀ "Take the mercy, accept the help" (Hebrews 4:16 MSG).

❀ "Be decent and true in everything you do"
   (Romans 13:13 TLB).

❀ "Don't fret or worry. Instead of worrying, pray"
   (Philippians 4:6 MSG).

❀ "Every cloud is a flag to your faithfulness"
   (Psalm 57:10 MSG).

❀ "Keep your mouth shut, and you will stay out of trouble"
   (Proverbs 21:23 NLT).

❀ "Guard against corruption from the godless world"
   (James 1:27 MSG).

❀ "A gentle tongue can break a bone" (Proverbs 25:15 NIV).

❀ "The fear of human opinion disables; trusting in GOD
   protects you from that" (Proverbs 29:25 MSG).

❀ "The secret things belong to the LORD our God" (Deuteronomy 29:29 NIV).

❀ "Why am I discouraged? Why is my heart so sad? I will put my hope in God!" (Psalm 43:5 NLT).

Why is it so important to ingest these Life Saver scriptures? Because you need to study the Bible yourself, not just accept what others have to say about it. Papa God wants to speak to *you* through His Word. They are personal messages, meant just for you. In the marvelously graphic words of my pastor, Mark Saunders, "Do you want to eat food that you've chewed or food that other people have chewed for you?"

I can promise you this, girlfriend: if you commit to devouring a Life Saver a month for just one year, you'll discover a new norm of power that will so eclipse your old wimpy way that you'll never go back. Say it with me: God's Word equals God's strength.

SOUL TENDING

Speaking of norms, my niece Andie will never be what most consider "normal." It'll always take her five times more effort and time than you or I to do even the simplest things, but she can certainly achieve the state of wellness, as in "It is well with my soul." Rick's sister-in-law may not regain complete physical health again in this world (although we pray she does), but even in the midst of her cancer battle, she may attain wellness. Soul wellness.

Let me explain.

The very essence of ourselves, the spiritual heart of the person our Creator meant for us to be, is referred to in Hebrew as *nepesh,* or our "soul."[5] In Deuteronomy 4:9, we're instructed to "keep your soul diligently" (NASB). That diligence is sometimes lost in our crazy-busy world, and our souls begin to run recklessly amok. Instead of being well nourished by our thriving, healthy, loving relationship with Papa God and watered daily by His Word, our soul can shrivel up from neglect.

Like that poor plant on your porch you've been meaning to tend to but somehow never got around to it. You're nodding your head right now, aren't you? Me, too.

How do we know if our soul is parched? If we're not clinging to Papa God as though our life depends on it, it most likely is. "I cling to you" (Psalm 63:8 NIV). Not unlike the symptoms of our pathetic plant's neglect, without our Source of sustenance we turn into brittle, wasted, dried-out twigs of apathy, weariness, and hopelessness. Am I describing you? I know I've recently been through a time when that pretty much described me. We all do.

But take heart, sister! Like the pathetic impatiens in my backyard that turn into shrink-dried, naked brown stalks in the sweltering heat of July but when watered liberally, miraculously raise their little heads, green up, spread their plump, rejuvenated arms, and bloom with bright colors once again, it's never too late for us to recover and thrive.

Not just live but *thrive*. (More on how to do this in chapter 22.)

I've always loved the words of that old hymn, "It Is Well with My Soul," written by Horatio Spafford, a wealthy Chicago lawyer and devout Christian whose only son died tragically at a young age. Not long afterward, Spafford lost nearly all his personal possessions and business investments in the Great Chicago Fire of 1871. Two years later, he was unexpectedly detained on last-minute business, so his wife and daughters, since they already had tickets, went ahead on a ship to England, where he would later join them. In a freak accident at sea, all four daughters drowned in the cold, watery depths. Yet somehow, after losing everything he once held dear, through Papa God's supernatural strength, Spafford was able to pen these incredible words:

When peace like a river attendeth my way,
When sorrows like sea billows roll;
Whatever my lot, Thou hast taught me to say,
It is well, it is well with my soul.

Wow. Snowball upside my head. Does the concept that we can attain wellness regardless of our circumstances wallop you as hard as it does me? Yet that's what almighty Yahweh can do for us. Wholeness when we're in pieces. Stability although we're fragmented. Restoration when we're broken.

Whatever my lot. . .*whatever* my lot, it is well with my soul.

I want to be able to sincerely say that, too. How about you? We can, you know, because Papa is walking with us, loving us, sharing His strength with us for every step of our journey. Stubbornness trenches and all.

If you're going through hell, keep going.
~WINSTON CHURCHILL

FOLLOWING MY PERSONAL GPS (GOD-POWERED SATELLITE)

1. Can you recall a time when someone came alongside and walked with you? What did this person's selfless actions mean to you?

2. Describe a time when you knew without a shadow of a doubt that Papa God was walking with you. How did you know? In what ways did He help you?

3. Second Corinthians 1:4 pretty much sums up our next assignment: "He brings us alongside someone else who is going through hard times so that we can be there for that person just as God was there for us" (MSG). Have you ever felt led to walk with someone who was experiencing difficulties? When? Did you feel depleted or invigorated by sharing your strength when he or she was weak?

4. How stocked is your spiritual pantry? Is your cupboard bare? Well then, how about some delicious Life Savers for the go-to shelf? (Put 'em beside the Oreos where they're easy to reach.) Tell you what, dear friend, if, or rather *when*, you begin savoring your Savers, I'd love to hear from you. Drop me a line at gracenotes@deboracoty.com and we'll swap some wild new flavors of the month even better than Chunky Monkey!

5. What about Horatio Spafford's story touches you most? So what do you think—

6. On a scale of one to ten, how well is your soul?

CHAPTER 5

Shine, Baby, Shine
(Love Lights Our Path)

Live a life filled with love,
following the example of Christ.
EPHESIANS 5:2 NLT

She'd done it all. Who could ask for more? My friend Tricia had lived the average American girl's wildest dream. During her years as a Playboy Bunny and later during a stint in Hollywood appearing in movies, she'd hobnobbed with the likes of Frank Sinatra, Harrison Ford, Tom Selleck, Henry Winkler, Jane Seymour, Tony Randall, and of course, Hugh Hefner.

She worked onstage in theater and as a television actress on shows like *The Fresh Prince of Bel Air*, *Roseanne*, *Cheers*; was featured in TV commercials; and yes, even appeared in the epitome of small screen success, *Seinfeld*. Tricia had all kinds of friends in high places. She was rich, beautiful, and famous. People adored her.

But it just wasn't enough.

Spiritually, she experienced a religious smorgasbord, dabbling in Catholicism, Protestantism, Mormonism, Buddhism, Hinduism, astral projection, and various New Age metaphysical pursuits. At one point in her long search for truth, she even channeled "ancient gods" (to misquote Shakespeare, demons by any other name would smell as rancid).

But despite all her effort to tap into the wisdom of the ages, Tricia found herself in her early forties unsettled, unfulfilled, and unhappy. Divorced and jaded, she had found nothing that could quench the deep, racking thirst within her for love. Real love. Forever love.

Then she met Jesus. A face-to-face encounter with nuclear blast love at ground zero.

I know that sounds a smidge cliché, but it's still true. Tricia was blown away by pure, never-changing-since-the-dawn-of-time, authentic love. And once Tricia devoted herself to the Lover of her soul, His incredible love permeated every area of her life, soaked her parched heart, and finally satiated that relentless thirst in her soul.

There are so many facets to love, aren't there? It's like a big flashy diamond on the hand of one of the glitzy ladies at one of Tricia's Hollywood parties; every way you turn love, it sparkles a little differently, reflecting the light shining upon it. Light, of course, is crucial to produce the sparkle. (If you've already figured out that the light in this metaphor represents someone whose name rhymes with Bod, you're three steps ahead and two to the right!)

Tricia's story touches on many of those sparkling facets. . .love for friends, family, self, lovers, the Almighty, that terrific movie you saw (or were in, in Tricia's case), your favorite jeans, to-die-for chocolate (did I mention Tricia is a choco-athelete like me?). But not all facets are equal. We can't really say, "I love Papa God" and "I love Godiva" are equivalent in their meanings, although to me, munching on a milk chocolate–layered wafer feels like an out-of-booty (oops, I mean body) experience.

No, the disparity in facets of love is a matter of depth and perspective. And we need to understand the differences.

You know, they say the Inuit (Eskimos) have thirty words for a single substance. Each denotes various colors, textures, and uses of the thing the rest of us know simply as ice. They differentiate because ice is of utmost importance to them, to their livelihood, to their very existence.

FOUR FACETS OF LOVE

The ancient Greeks had numerous words for love. I like to think that's because love was crucial to them, to their livelihood, to their very existence. Just like it is to me today. Just like it is to you. So since love is so über important to us (and the topic of this book), let's take a few moments to review the four facets of love we find in the Bible.

❀ Agape: love in the deepest spiritual sense; selfless love not dependent on circumstances or fleeting feelings. It's commitment to seek the very best for the other person, regardless of emotion.

Agapao or agape love is generated by the lover, not the one loved; it's sacrificial love that expects nothing in return. Used over three hundred times in the New Testament alone, agape expresses the unconditional love of our Creator for us and the selfless love He asks us to extend to His other creations. Even the unlovable ones.

It can be found in passages like John 3:16, "For God so loved [agape] the world that He gave His only begotten Son, that whoever believes in Him should not perish but have everlasting life" (NKJV) and Matthew 5:44, "But I say to you, love [agape] your enemies, bless those who curse you, do good to those who hate you, and pray for those who spitefully use you and persecute you" (NKJV).

When you think about it, agape love—the supernatural type of love originating from Papa God that He offers to share with us in forging our relationships with other people—is the *only* way we can love those prickly people we simply don't like. It requires no response on their part and basically says, "I choose to love you, regardless of your feelings or actions toward me." (I really want to add at the end of that sentence, ". . .you weaseling warthog!" but let's not.)

The old saying is true: You can forgive someone without loving them, but you can't love someone without forgiving them.

❁ Eros: the euphoric sensation of love. The fireworks, bells, and whistles.

Our word *erotic* comes from the same root, although eros doesn't include actual sex acts. It's the internal mind-generated feelings, not the external aftermath. It's raw, passionate emotion. On the strength scale, eros can be interpreted as more than philia (we'll get to that next) but less than agape. Eros is often the romantic emotion of love without the balance of logic, like "love at first sight."

Whereas agape is you-centered, eros is me-centered, as in "I love you because you bring me pink roses and mint and dark chocolate–swirl Dove bars." (I personally believe Cupid melts these irresistible choco-aphrodisiacs and dips the tips of his arrows in them.)

The word *eros* doesn't appear in the Bible but is implied as the emotional element of love—the nervous, exciting, sweaty, heart-racing romantic attraction between a man and woman, like the hots Samson had for Delilah (Judges 16) or what Boaz felt when he awoke to find Ruth lying at his feet (Ruth 2–4). (Hard to fathom how lying at a guy's feet would light his fire, but hey, they say men are dry twigs in a match factory.)

I'm tempted to add David's rooftop passion for Bathsheba here, but that's really more lust than love, which falls in a different category—the Greek term *mania*, which indicates desire mixed with greed and obsession. In my opinion that isn't really love at all.

The thing to remember about eros is that because it's based on emotion, it can change at the drop of a hormone. And as women hard-wired with overwhelming, rationale-domineering emotion, we can certainly understand how unstable and unpredictable eros love can be without the stabilizing force of phila.

❀ Phila: the affection found in friendship.

Phila grows and deepens with time. This steady type of love is based on loyalty and commitment rather than sentiment. *Phileo* or phila is found between family members and friends and can also mean fondness of a particular food, item, or activity, as in "I love (phila) whacking the stuffing out of a tennis ball in Philadelphia (the city of brotherly love)." I suspect for most gals it would be correct to say, "I love (phila) ooey, gooey triple chocolate chunk brownies," but for me, it definitely falls into the hyper realm of eros. (Pausing now to wipe drool off the page.)

Phila is used in Romans 12:10, "Love [phila] each other as brothers and sisters and honor others more than you do yourself" (CEV) and 1 Peter 1:22, "You must keep on loving (phila) with all your heart" (CEV).

❀ Storge: the intimate relationship generally attributed to parents and their offspring, as in "motherly love."

This type of love is strong and resilient but at the same time lopsided and unequal; it's based on the dependency of the weaker individual on the stronger and can therefore sometimes result in maltreatment. This storge (pronounced "stor-gay" like the hard *g* in agape) type of love can be toxic when transferred into marriage, whereas in healthy relationships, eros attracts and phila is the glue that keeps couples together.

Like eros, storge is not found verbatim in the Bible, but

examples are abundant. For instance, Noah's relationship with his sons and their wives (Genesis 6–9) and Isaac and Rebecca's love for their twins, Jacob and Esau (Genesis 25:28). Of course the standout New Testament example of storge love in its purest, holiest form is Mary's unwavering devotion to her Son, Jesus, from the manger to the cross and beyond.

Basking in Love's Glow

Just marveling about the sparkling facets of love can bring luminosity to your face, can't it? And we don't need to be in the presence of a star like Tricia's buds Tom Selleck or Harrison Ford to reflect the light! Why, it's downright mind-boggling pondering the ins and outs of Papa God's vast love for us. His love is:

Incredible	Outrageous
Inescapable	Outpouring
Inexhaustible	Outlandish
Inexplicable	Outclassable
Indestructible	Outstanding

Before I close this chapter on the power of love, I want to stop right now and take the opportunity to hit my knees and pray for you, dear sister, to be bathed in the glow of love's many facets. I echo Paul's letter to the believers at Ephesus (Ephesians 3:17–19 NLT) in my heartfelt prayer for you:

> May your roots go down deep into
> the soil of God's marvelous love.
> And may you have the power to understand,
> as all God's people should,

how wide,
how long,
how high,
and how deep
His love really is.
May you experience the love of Christ,
Though it is so great you will never fully understand it.
Then you will be filled with the fullness of life and power
that comes from Papa God.
Amen.

It is a risk to love. What if it doesn't work out? Ah, but what if it does.
~PETER MCWILLIAMS

FOLLOWING MY PERSONAL GPS (GOD-POWERED SATELLITE)

1. What is most memorable for you about Tricia's story? How does it compare to your own searching-for-love experience?

2. Describe a time in your life when you were touched by agape love from the Lord. Can you think of a time you were able to extend agape love to a warthog (I mean an enemy)?

3. Okay, time for fun. Think back on one of your fondest romantic memories of eros love. Now spill. Inquiring minds want to know. (Remember, eros is *not* physical sex acts; let's keep this rated PG.)

4. First, tell about your fave edible target for phila love. Now a human phila target—who is your all-time BFF? Why? (I hope she's sitting beside you right now so she can hear this!)

5. Who are the recipients of your storge (motherly) love? If you're not a mom, no worries. It doesn't have to be *your* kids; it can be someone else's for whom you feel a strong attachment or protectiveness. And hey, many people feel storge love for their four-legged children, too (mine's a miniature poodle named Fenway!).

CHAPTER 6

He's Got My Whole World in His Hands
(Gaining Confidence)

————————❋————————

How priceless is your unfailing love, O God!
PSALM 36:7 NIV

|||||||||||||||||||||||||||||||||||||||||||||||||||||||||||||||||||||||||||||||||||||||||||||||||||||||||||||||||

I arrived a few minutes early at the hotel conference room for the all-day continuing education course, just in time to grab a cup of hot tea from the back of the room and find a seat. (I never quit my day job when I started writing professionally a decade ago, so I still maintain my occupational therapy license, thirty-five years and counting).

To my surprise, I ran into an acquaintance with whom I'd worked years before. April and I were never bosom buddies, for she was all about the external and I was more about the internal. April was not at all interested in spiritual things and was the trendy, designer-clad, status type, while I was more polyester blue light special. Still, we had been cordial from our different stratospheres, so since I knew no one else there, I asked if we could sit together.

"Um, I guess so," she replied after a brief hesitation (I somehow missed the red flag flapping in my face here). I noticed she was wearing very "in" sleek black spandex yoga togs with a breezy gray over-blouse barely concealing her slim, hard-bodied torso. I was wearing comfortably saggy Kmart jeans. And a floppy hat.

Can you say, "Happy have-not"?

"Jill is coming, and we're going to sit together. But I suppose you can join us, too," April said with a strange little catch in her voice. Jill was an amiable previous coworker, too, so I naively thought this boring day was suddenly looking up.

I followed April to a table near the front and sat on her left, while Jill rushed in a few minutes later to sit on her right. While I was greeting Jill, I noticed an odd thing happening to April's chair in between us. It gradually scooted more and more to the right, so that by the time the instructor began talking, April was facing Jill with her back to me. And there she remained throughout the rest of the day, effectively blocking me out of their conversation and reminding me in no uncertain body language that I was a boil on her behunkus. A black fly in the strawberry yogurt. A zit on picture day.

I didn't know if April was afraid that my "religious persuasion" might somehow stomp on her spiritual toes or if she was disgusted by my fashion sense. But whatever the reason, I suddenly felt invisible.

SHEDDING THE INVISIBILITY CLOAK

It's a sad but true fact that we inevitably will face times in this life when we feel invisible—like our presence counts for nothing. Our opinions might actually be briefly entertained and our actions superficially acknowledged, but in the end, we are wholly ignored. No one involved cares what we think, feel, or do. We create no ripple. It's as if we don't even exist.

Even we happy have-nots detest being invisible, don't we? Everyone needs to feel significant. So here are four visibility tips I'd like to share with you that I've been working on implementing more effectively during the past few years.

❀ Take steps to improve your self-confidence. Remember, you're not merely a have-not. . .you're a will-be! Eleanor Roosevelt said, "No one can make you feel inferior without your consent."

When April rejected me at the conference, I'll admit my first reaction was self-incrimination. I somehow felt I deserved to be dissed because I was in a lower chic strata. But then I sprouted a backbone. I reminded myself that designerless clothing and goofy hat or not, I'm a child of the King and therefore a princess in my own right. A little positive self-talk goes a long way. (More on this important topic in the "Toxic Voices" chapter of my book *Fear, Faith, and a Fistful of Chocolate*.)

I silently lectured myself that Papa knows I have oodles of worth and has gifted me with specific skills that many folks find edifying. One of these is the gift of acceptance. I can befriend a stinkbug. (Unless, apparently, its name is April.)

There had to be someone in that room who would be uplifted by a friendly conversation.

So as soon as the first break rolled around, I chatted up the gal sitting behind me and then another at the coffee table. We found lots to laugh about together, these new girlfriends and I, and the whole morning grew bright and cheerful. As W. C. Fields once droned in his nasally voice, "It ain't what they call you, it's what you answer to."

❀ Be aware of your body language. Confident people don't slouch, hunch, or keep their eyes lowered to the ground (or glued to their iPhones). They stand upright and look others in the eyes.

Sloppy posture says more about you than you may realize. Whether you intend to or not, the way you carry yourself and the smile (or scowl) on your face announces to people how you feel about yourself. My rule of thumb: pretend that you're wearing an invisible tiara. You'll stand tall to keep it from falling off, and you'll automatically morph to daughter-of-the-King mode. Not in a haughty way but by exemplifying kindness, graciousness, and confidence. Like lovely Princess Kate, who's got nothing on you, girlfriend (except maybe a million dollars and a prince to whip at croquet).

I was fascinated by a scene in the 2000 made-for-TV movie about the life of Audrey Hepburn. Jennifer Love Hewitt played the lead with all the elegance, beauty, and grace exuded by the real Audrey. In this memorable scene, after she was awarded the 1953 best actress Oscar for *Roman Holiday*, Audrey made a statement to the press and added a personal note that went something like this: "I want to thank my mother, who taught me to walk and sit erect. . .it has made me what I am today."

Wow. If that's not an effective endorsement for practicing good posture, I'm the dot at the bottom of a question mark. I saw that flick over a decade ago and have never forgotten that statement. I think about it whenever I find myself sitting at my computer curved into, well, a question mark.

❧ Don't stoop to condescension if the stiletto shifts to the other foot. Revenge is ugly. When you act confident around people who have dismissed or overlooked you, be careful not to yield to the temptation to retaliate.

During our last break at the conference, a fellow walked over to my table and asked if I was "that author whose books my wife loves so much." He'd recognized the name on my chest ("Hello.

My Name Is. . ."). April blatantly eavesdropped as he related how much my books meant to his wife and that she had bought copies for all her friends.

As soon as he walked away, April, still gaping at me in unabashed flabbergastation asked, "What—are you famous or something?" I assured her I was not, but a funny thing happened. I noticed that she began to ease her chair back in my direction for the meeting's final minutes.

As if I actually mattered. I was suddenly visible.

When we were dismissed, I really wanted to snark, "Well, April, it was lovely staring at the back of your head today," but I knew that no useful purpose would be served (except to placate my latent vindictiveness) and it would certainly make Papa frown. So I muttered my Life Saver of the month to myself, "Be decent and true in everything you do. . ." (Romans 13:13 TLB), and kept my sassy mouth shut.

I don't need revenge nearly as much as I need love.

❀ Be an active listener. Confident people don't need to hog attention by doing all the talking. Nor do they zone out while someone else is spilling. They are 100 percent present and make the other person feel wanted and appreciated by attentively listening, responding, and acting interested.

Now I know active listening is *not* easy; with a nanosecond attention span, I struggle with it constantly. But it does get easier. A trick I learned long ago is to focus on the other person's nasal hairs while they speak; the follicle movement forces you to stay in the moment and keeps your attention riveted, especially if allergies have added a mucus glisten. Plus, in some strangely twisted way it makes you feel more intimately acquainted.

DELILAH LOVE IS ALL ABOUT DE LIE

We've all experienced times when we feel horrifically unlovely and will likely experience more before the fat lady sings. There will be lonely, deflating, ego-shattering days when we wonder why the Lord isn't paying attention to the angst of His disrespected daughter. Is He on vacation in Tahiti? Did our misery slip past Him when He yawned? Maybe He doesn't really care about us all that much, we stew. After all, nobody else seems to.

When we don't feel loved by our fellow creations, it's easy to fall into the stinkin' thinkin' of not feeling loved by our Creator as well. But did you catch the operative word here? Feel. We don't *feel* loved. The kicker is that emotion is not factual. Just because we don't feel something doesn't mean it isn't there. Conversely, feeling something doesn't make it true.

Case in point: I was crazy in love with Joey in the tenth grade. He was a football hunk with mambo lips and Fabio hair. All the girls swooned over him (long locks on males were hip back then). I got to sit by him for a whole hour in fourth-period English. I constantly daydreamed about the blissful day he'd finally realize I was the woman for him, so I doodled "Joey" all over my notebook covers in fat curlicue letters and even sported a colorful marker-etched Joey tattoo on my wrist. I was fully convinced that I could never, ever love anyone more than I loved Joey.

Then one day, Joey got a haircut. Whoa. Like sheared biblical Samson, he suddenly lost all power. At least his power over me.

The moment I saw Joey's newly shorn head, my great, all-consuming, forever kind of love. . .simply. . .[*poof*] vanished. I was shocked that the deepest of all possible loves could just throw itself off a cliff in sixty short seconds, but even in my shallow, immature state, I did learn something about feelings that day. They're tricky little devils. You can't trust 'em.

REALITY SEEMS SO. . .REAL

Emotions may feel strong and powerful and ever so real, but they're not the basis of truth. In fact, they're often the basis of false reality. We base our perception of the world on our feelings, which tend to bend like a sapling in the stiff breezes of change.

Now, forty years later with a tad more maturity under the bridge, I realize it's actually the other way around. Truth is the basis of bottom-line reality. And this reality should be the catalyst for our feelings. What truth am I talking about? What reality? The truth that:

❀ Papa God is love (1 John 4:8).

❀ He chooses to lavish His love upon His devoted children (1 John 3:1).

❀ His love is unfailing (Psalm 36:7).

❀ Because of Papa's abundant love, He shows us grace and compassion (Jonah 4:2).

❀ He will never leave us or forsake us (Hebrews 13:5).

Nope. Never. Not even when we doubt. Or run away. Or hide. Not during the awful times when we don't feel loved. Or accepted. Or even tolerated. I've said this before, and I'll say it again: Whether we feel His love or not, it's still there for us all along. Like the love we feel for our toddler when he's sitting in time-out and doesn't feel at all loved.

Strong, meaningful love, able to lift us up from the pond scum of self-depreciating lies in which we wallow.

So get up. Stand erect. Wipe the slime off your knickers. Put on your goofiest hat and your cheesiest jeans. And smile. You're loved beyond all comprehension. You're Someone's favorite person in the whole wide world.

Now *that's* reality, sister.

> *[Confidence] is 50 percent what you've got and*
> *50 percent what people think you've got.*
>
> ~SOPHIA LOREN

FOLLOWING MY PERSONAL GPS (GOD-POWERED SATELLITE)

1. Which do you think is worse—to be scrutinized and rejected or ignored and invisible?

2. Which of the above scenarios happens to you most often? Why do you think that is?

3. Browse through some photos, or better yet, videos of yourself. What does your body language say about how you feel about yourself? In what way does how you feel affect how you look? Does it work in reverse, too—does how you look affect how you feel?

4. Author Richard Kline said, "Confidence is preparation." How would you rate your confidence level in a new environment— say, a room full of strangers at a party—on a one (low) to ten (high) scale? Brainstorm how you could raise that number by better preparation.

5. In what setting do you feel the most confident? Least confident? What are you basing that number on—appearance, self-esteem, job, kids, achievements, social position, marital status. . .or something else? What *should* your confidence be based on?

SECTION 2

Can Anyone Really Refold Maps?

This is how everyone will recognize that you are my disciples— when they see the love you have for each other.
JOHN 13:35 MSG

CHAPTER 7

Raise Your Hand if You Need a Do-Over
(Rebooting for a Fresh Start)

Anyone who belongs to Christ has become a new person
The old life is gone; a new life has begun!
2 Corinthians 5:17 NLT

Remember the scene in Billy Crystal's popular 1991 film *City Slickers* when Billy's character, Mitch, is trying to encourage his down-in-the-dumps lifelong pal Phil (played by Daniel Stern)? The guys are herding cattle from New Mexico to Colorado in a desperate midlife crisis attempt to find themselves.

I guess guyfriends need girlfriend getaways, too. Keeps the bromance alive.

Anyway, due to his own rotten choices, Phil has just lost his wife, his job, and what little security he's ever had. He feels completely hopeless. Wasted. Mitch reminds him of their childhood games when a ball would get stuck up in a tree and someone would yell, "Do-over!"

"Now you have a chance to start over," Mitch tells Phil. "You've got a clean slate." Phil isn't buying it at the moment, but after a series of near-death, crazy-funny experiences (in a way only Billy Crystal can make near-death experiences crazy-funny), Phil decides to embrace the hope offered by that clean slate. As he says good-bye to Mitch at the airport, Phil admits, "My life is a do-over; it's time to get started."

Renovatio is Latin for "a total rebirth," meaning to cast off the old and embrace the new. Just add an *n* on the end and you have *renovation*. And that's what many of us yearn for—a life reno. But change can be hard. Very hard. Even if it's change for the better. Let's face it, the only person who likes change is a baby with a wet diaper. In the vernacular of youth, flux sucks.

But sometimes renovatio is exactly what we need.

JIMMY'S DO-OVER

My friend Jimmy knows the incredible power of renovatio. He once was highly respected in his community, held public office, rubbed shoulders with governors, and was in charge of the entire state prison system. But that was before he found himself on the wrong side of the bars.

Jimmy's fall was shattering. But his life reno was wondrous.

The need to attain success was always the motivating force in Jimmy's life. He simply had to be the best. The top dog. The dude in charge. In Jimmy's words, "My ego would accept nothing less." Above all else, he yearned to be seen as important. To be respected and admired.

Sound familiar? Isn't that what you and I want, too?

Throughout his school years, Jimmy learned that the best way to win people over was to be friendly, do favors, and pretend to be a good boy. Then they were putty in your hands. The lesson stuck.

After college, he discovered that he could best appease his greed for power through politics. So he poured his energies into being elected to the city commission then mayor of his small town. He and his wife Leslie and two children attended church every Sunday because that's what good Southerners do. Plus it was a great way to snag votes.

Faith was a part of Jimmy's life on the outside but not on the inside. He had walked the aisle during a revival at age seven after a fire-and-brimstone sermon about hell scared him spitless. He told the preacher that he loved Jesus and was baptized without understanding or embracing what it meant to truly give your heart to the Lord; he was simply escaping hell. Nothing much changed inside of Jimmy after he came up from the baptismal waters. It meant more to his family than it did to him. As Jimmy so aptly puts it, "I was just a wet kid."

Being raised by devout Christian parents, Jimmy grew up in church, learning the correct rhetoric and playing the role that was expected of him. But he never had a real relationship with Christ. Then he married Leslie, a beautiful, faith-filled woman, and after they began their family, they agreed that bringing up their children in the church was the right thing to do.

They appeared to be the ideal Christian family. He'd become adept at fooling everyone.

Jimmy's day job was working for the state's Department of Corrections. Although he'd climbed to the lofty rank of warden, it wasn't enough. That insatiable ego clamored for more. He set his sights on the highest state position in his field. It was a red-letter day when Jimmy received the call from the governor offering him a seat on his cabinet as secretary of the Department of Corrections. He would be the head honcho. The top banana. Jimmy would be responsible for twenty-five thousand state employees in seventy institutions, and a 2.5 billion dollar budget.

His dream had come true. Jimmy had reached his lifetime goal. Looking back, Jimmy reflects, "I thought I would finally be important and my ego would be satisfied. But it wasn't. I just couldn't figure out why I still felt so empty."

When the small-town country boy moved to the large, bustling state capital, people crept out of the woodwork—professional ego-stroking people—who called themselves friends. Friends who offered gifts and cash and wonderful trips for a bit of influence on how that 2.5 billion would be spent.

At first he dug in his heels and resisted what he knew wasn't right, but over a two-year period, Jimmy gradually skidded down the slippery slope inch by inch. It's called accepting kickbacks and is a violation of federal law. Jimmy learned he was being investigated by the FBI, and the pressure mounted. Although it wasn't public knowledge and he'd admitted his guilt to no one—not even Leslie—he knew the truth would eventually be exposed.

Time dragged. The wait was pure torture. His days were filled with fear and dread. When would the hammer fall?

Then one September morning in 2005, he could no longer bear the burden alone. His defenses crashed and burned. Sinking to his knees beside his bed, Jimmy tearfully poured out his heart to Almighty God. . .remorse for all the pain he'd caused those he loved, lies and more lies, his greed for power, the deceit and self-serving that had controlled his life. Everything.

He laid his ego on the altar of ash he'd made of his life.

Jimmy admitted that he'd had enough of doing things his way and needed a fresh start. From his church days, Jimmy knew the Bible and the teachings of Jesus in considerable detail. But he had never really believed God's Word was the truth. The *only* truth. The *only* way. But on that day, at that moment, Jimmy made the decision to believe. Wholeheartedly. To hold nothing back but put all his chips on the table and cash in with Jesus.

The old Jimmy facade was shattered. But through the shards of his brokenness, renovatio began.

While Jimmy knew he was forgiven by God, he was certainly not forgiven by man. Violating the public trust carried serious consequences. Jimmy's first real test as a new Christian came when the political guillotine dropped four months later.

Busted. Headlines. Newscasts.

A media feeding frenzy made him notorious. Public enemy number one. His face and disgrace were plastered everywhere. How would he react? Would he tell the truth? Could he, for the first time in his life, not resort to lies to cover his sins and trust the Lord to take care of him no matter what? Would Yahweh really provide peace despite the shame of public humiliation, failure, desertion by those he'd thought were friends, and even imprisonment for his crimes?

By the mercy of Jesus, the answer to all those questions was a resounding yes.

The year between entering his guilty plea with the federal magistrate and his sentencing was the most emotionally difficult in Jimmy's life. But his faith walk was only just beginning. After running prisons for thirty years, he was about to become a prisoner himself.

Jimmy was sentenced to eight years in federal prison. *Eight years.*

That time turned out to be the proving ground for Jimmy's new faith. God began to work double time in his life. Through one miracle after another, the prison became Jimmy's personal seminary and monastery all rolled up into one. His relationship with his Savior grew and deepened as he seriously delved into the Bible to complete his doctorate in theology. He felt less fear and greater peace than he had in his entire life.

YOUR DO-OVER CAN HAVE
A HAPPY ENDING, TOO

Through all this time, Leslie was Jimmy's rock. She not only forgave him and agreed to try to save their marriage, but Leslie and their daughter also drove the twenty-eight-hour round-trip to visit and support Jimmy countless times. They spent many hours sitting together, discussing the Lord's fingerprints on their lives and how He had pulled their fragmented family back together. To this day, Leslie considers herself immensely blessed. "I have never in my life seen change in a person like I have seen in Jimmy. God has humbled him, taught him, and used him for His glory, and we pray daily that He will continue to use him and guide us both as we live a life of obedience in Christ."

Five and a half years after the gates clanged shut behind him, Jimmy was released early to house arrest and probation. A new man. It was the biggest miracle of all: the chance to start over as a new creature in Christ.

But who on earth would employ a sixty-year-old ex-con? In divine irony (don't you love Papa God's sense of humor?), as soon as the prison exit door smacked his back pockets, Jimmy was invited to teach a seminary class on the epistles Paul wrote from prison. I mean, really, who could have a better perspective of *that*?

And shortly thereafter, Jimmy was asked to join the administrative staff of a church led by a pastor, who when asked why he would even consider hiring an ex-criminal, simply smiled, shrugged, and replied, "We're about grace."

All Christ-emulators should be about grace, don't you think? Grace—undeserved kindness—is the bottom line of do-overs. And as a bonus, Papa's grace toward us rolls over into our grace toward others who need a reno, too.

You can start over right where you are. Right now. Your spiritual GPS can recalculate a new direction. Renovatio, baby. It's possible. It's doable. It's do-overable. And that do-over hovering on your horizon is oozing with hope.

This is not the beginning of a new chapter in my life;
this is the beginning of a new book! That first book is already closed,
ended, and tossed into the seas; this new book is newly opened,
has just begun! Look, it is the first page! And it's a beautiful one!
~ JOYBELL C.

FOLLOWING MY PERSONAL GPS (GOD-POWERED SATELLITE)

1. There's tremendous power in a do-over. Can you think of an example in the life of someone where Papa God disarmed the destructive and poisonous grip the past had over them and the Holy Spirit breathed in new life, purpose, and hope?

2. Right after Jesus delivered the beloved John 3:16 passage (stop a moment and recite it. I know you remember: "For God so loved the world. . ."), He then lovingly said, "There is no judgment against anyone who believes in him [Jesus, the only Son of God]" (John 3:18 NLT). What does that scripture tell you about condemnation for your past mistakes?

3. What about guilt? Do you ever struggle with guilt over things you've screwed up. . .people you've hurt. . .poor choices you've made? Here are two verses releasing you from guilt you can look up and add to your Life Saver list: Romans 8:1 and Hebrews 8:12. Read them aloud slowly, contemplating each word. Now ditch the guilt like those purple platform heels you've been meaning to toss. If you're not sure how, check out my *Fear, Faith, and a Fistful of Chocolate* chapter about guilt called, "Had Your Vitamin G Today?"

4. What is "God's gift" in Romans 5:16? "God's gift made it possible for us to be acceptable to him, even though we have sinned many times" (CEV). How important is it to you to be acceptable to the final Judge of all mankind?

5. Feeling the need for a do-over? A little personal reno of your own? In which area of your life? No time like the present to start! Papa's grace is right there for the taking—just reach out and embrace it.

CHAPTER 8

He Loves Me, He Loves Me More
(Learning to Feel Cherished)

Thank you for making me so wonderfully complex!
Your workmanship is marvelous— how well I know it.
You watched me as I was being formed. . .
You saw me before I was born. . . .
How precious are your thoughts about me, O God!
PSALM 139:14–17 NLT

Everybody said it wouldn't be bad at all. Piece of cake. No problemo. They'll knock you out and the painless procedure will be over so quickly you'll wonder if you ever had a colonoscopy at all, they said. It's a completely routine medical procedure these days, they said. No muss. . .no fuss. . .no sweat.

And I believed them.

But I was wrong. Drag up a stool (nasty pun intended) and I'll tell you all about my colonoscopy from Hades.

The clincher (a little sphincter humor there) is that I wouldn't have known about any of it if my blood pressure hadn't tanked after the nurse injected my first little dab of woozy juice. Because my BP flatlined at 80/40 and the infrastructure had already been breached (meaning the little camera gizmo was already on its way through the maze that was my guts), they couldn't give me more sedative until my BP crept higher. It never did. Therefore, I was

100 percent awake and ever-so-reluctantly alert throughout the entire ill-fated procedure.

So there I was lying on my side watching a red-tinted version of *Journey to the Center of the Earth* on the monitor, only this time it was *Journey to the Center of My Girth*. My bare tush was protruding from the hospital gown and blanket that covered the rest of my shivering body in the subzero room, as the male and female MDs took turns guiding the little inner-spaceship through the tight, twisting tunnel that was my colon.

About ten minutes into it, I felt a sudden jerk on the camera tether, followed by a strange *thwomp* sound behind me.

"What was that?" I asked the nurse sitting on a rolling stool in front of me, monitoring my BP. She rose to her feet and peered over my backside, her eyes growing wide as trashcan lids.

"Um, I think we're going to have a slight delay," she said, forgetting to close her mouth after the last word.

"What do you mean?" I asked, feeling the little inner space vessel turn upside down and ram into my spleen. Or maybe my bladder.

I knew something was clearly amiss when someone began repeating over the intercom system, "Code Blue, Code Blue, Code Blue," in a rushed, high-pitched voice.

Now, I didn't know what Code Blue was, but obviously it was not a normal thing. Or a good thing either, by the way worried-looking people in scrubs rushed into the room and gathered at the exact location of my birthday-suited bum.

Chuck, in the waiting room just down the hall, heard the code and couldn't help but notice all the brouhaha involving the same door he'd seen me disappear behind earlier. You'd think he'd be sprouting an ulcer, right? Hardly. He admits that his first thought was, *Oh, great. What's Deb done now?*

The man's been married to me entirely too long.

Turns out the female doctor navigating the camera fainted. Yep. Passed out. *Thud*. Right on the floor. In the middle of my colonoscopy. (Rumor had it she was acutely pregnant.) The show ground to a halt as the smelling salts were broken out and a little impromptu tea party took place within inches of my naked derri-ere. In an act of good will, I chimed in and offered a peppermint from my purse in yonder locker if it would help. Nobody bit.

As they helped the stricken doc out the door, she mouthed a silent, "I'm so sorry" in my direction. *Not as sorry as I am*, I thought. *Nothing like southern exposure to humble one. Everybody in this zip code has now been up close and personal with my hind quarter cellulite.*

But the show must go on. So the male MD took over. With a vengeance. I don't know if he was trying to make up for lost time, or if his breakfast burrito had too many chili peppers, but he was jamming that joystick, baby, full speed ahead. And I felt every speed bump, crook, and cranny. Why on earth Papa God has to put so many sensory receptors where the sun doesn't shine, I'll never know, but I was ooooh-ing and whooaaa-ing with more and more intensity when we suddenly encountered the first ninety-degree turn.

Try as it might, my little inner-space traveler could not stay on the road to make that sharp angle. During the third effort to muscle through the curve, I arched off the table with an honest-to-goodness scream and the doc decided to call it a crash and burn. The mission was aborted. The ship returned to the launchpad.

THINK CHERISH, NOT PERISH

Now if you're of a certain age, please don't use my story as an excuse to forego your overdue colonoscopy. . .you must realize this whole bizarre thing was a complete fluke. I have come to accept my lot in life as one who hears at least once a week, "Oh my goodness—that's never happened before!" or "I can't believe this! I've worked here thirty years and have never seen such a thing!"

I believe it's the sly sense of humor harbored by the Creator of heaven and mirth. He's creatively providing fodder for my writing, which I was lured into by well-meaning people who repeatedly coerced, "Wow—what a crazy story! Who would believe it? You should write that down!"

But you know what it really shows me? That I'm unique in Papa God's eyes. I'm special. I'm cherished. Precious are His thoughts about me (Psalm 139:17). He understands me so well that He knows sometimes I just need something out of the ordinary and utterly ridiculous to jolt me out of my stupor. Something to awaken my paralyzed senses to begin seeing and feeling and living vibrantly in the moment again, rather than just numbly going through the paces of life stuck in the joy-sucking dully-funks.

It's never His intention to harm me but always to benefit me. "For I know the plans I have for you," declares the Lord, "plans to prosper you and not to harm you, plans to give you hope and a future" (Jeremiah 29:11 NIV). Plans for everyday living to be an exciting adventure, not a dull drudgery. Plans for His baby girl Debora to enjoy the gift of life to its fullest as a beloved child of the one true King.

And what applies to me applies to you, girlfriend. Papa God wants you to live abundantly, too. Why, He might even send you your own brand of zany adventures. Oh, yeah. Like driving away a two hundred–pound bear from your kitchen door with a fourteen-inch zucchini.[6]

Or accidentally falling onto the highway while trying to go potty in the bathroom in a motor home traveling down an interstate.[7]

Or suddenly remembering that Grandma's ashes are stored in the silk violet vase you sold to a stranger at your garage sale for two dollars.[8]

Or accidentally driving your car off a rural road and being surrounded by a herd of hip-tall enamored hogs that refuse to leave.[9]

Yep, all these things actually happened to real women (thankfully, they weren't me!). I'll bet a few radically bodacious things have happened to you, too, when you've needed jarring from your own mundane dully-funks. (Hey, I'd love to hear about them!) Only goes to show that Papa God intimately cares about every detail of your life and will do anything it takes to root out the best *you* possible.

Making a Love List. Checking It Twice.

Here are some of my favorite pieces of evidence depicting Papa God's immense, soul-soaking, boundary-less love for us. The kicker is. . .they're all from just two chapters of a single book of the Bible— 1 John in the New Testament (c'mon grab your Bible, look up the verses, and follow along with me). I call them my 1 John Love List:

❀ He considers us His beloved children (1 John 3:1).

❀ Our sins are lovingly forgiven by Him if we repent (1 John 3:5).

❀ When it comes to love, actions do speak louder than words (1 John 3:18).

❀ Papa God knows everything in our hearts (1 John 3:20).

❀ He gives us confidence (1 John 3:21).

❀ He intercedes to help us win our battles (1 John 4:4).

❀ He helps us love the unlovable (1 John 4:7).

❀ His passion for us is so enormous, He sent His precious only Son to die in our place so that we could live with Him forever (1 John 4:9).

❀ He is the embodiment of true love and is happy to fill us with that love until we're overflowing (1 John 4:12).

❀ We no longer have to be afraid, because His love is strong enough to overpower all fear (1 John 4:18).

Whoa. If this many assurances of Papa's vast love for us explode from merely two pages of the Bible, just think how loved we'll feel after reading the whole thing!

Want to know a great way to keep these awesome truths from getting buried in the avalanche of day-to-day bills, chores, obligations, and appointments? It's a simple but immensely effective trick I learned ten years ago from a marriage seminar. Chuck and I bought little plastic heart-shaped pink bracelets (they come in a multipack at the dollar store) to leave hidden around the house for each other to find as a tangible reminder of the playful side of our love for each other (it's especially effective for those times you'd rather strangle than wrangle).

Fun never gets old! We're still hiding them all these years later.

It worked so well, I bought little blue shiny heart bracelets as a symbol of Papa's deep affection for me. . .a mobile testament that I'm cherished even during the rabble of every day. I leave them for myself in places I frequent—in the fridge beside the Diet Coke, my nail polish drawer, atop my hidden Cadbury stash—to bring a smile to my face and joy to my weary heart when they remind me of Papa's lovin'. Or more like love-*un*. . .love that's unending, unqualified, unconditional, and unequaled.

Sometimes we girls need tangible reminders of the intangibles that keep us going on tough days. Otherwise, when the doctor faints, or the grizzlies drop in for a latte, or we logroll onto the interstate clutching a roll of toilet paper, we'll wrap up in the mudroom rag rug like a giant wiener and hide ourselves in the closet behind Mr. Hoover.

And nobody wants to be a whiny weenie.

Forget love—I'd rather fall in chocolate!
~SANDRA J. DYKES

✦ FOLLOWING MY PERSONAL GPS
(GOD-POWERED SATELLITE)

1. What unique wake-up call has Papa God used to jolt you from the dully-funks? (Hopefully it has nothing to do with bear-bopping zucchini!)

2. Flip back to the first truth on the 1 John Love List: "He considers us His beloved children." How does the way Papa feels about you relate to the way you feel about your children?

3. Does having an intimate part in their conception and care give you a special bond with your children? How would you feel if they went days or even weeks without communicating with you? How do you think Papa God feels when we do that to Him?

4. "Papa God knows everything in our hearts." Whoa. That's heavy, isn't it? Stop a moment and consider some of your secret thoughts that you're glad nobody else knows. But wait—Someone does know! How does 1 John 3:20 (fourth on the 1 John Love List) affect you?

5. What kind of memory-jogger would work for you, like my little blue hearts work for me? You know—something to signify Papa's love-*un* for you. (Don't forget to move your little love tokens around to new hiding places whenever you find one.)

CHAPTER 9

Dancing to Grace Notes
(Recognizing Everyday Miracles)

*God rewrote the text of my life when I opened
the book of my heart to his eyes.*
Psalm 18:24 msg

‖‖‖

My friend Cheryl was pushing her baby in a stroller down a quiet suburban sidewalk when she suddenly saw a pit bull running toward her with a rope tied around his neck. She'd seen the dog before, secured to a tree behind a neighbor's house on another street and heard he was restrained because of his unpredictable aggressive tendencies.

He'd apparently broken loose. And he was headed right for her.

Panicked, Cheryl had no time to formulate a plan; the big dog was closing in fast. She shot up a rhino-in-the-road prayer for protection and with her heart in her throat, threw herself in front of the stroller as a human shield, bracing for the attack.

Just as the dog drew near to Cheryl and her baby, he passed by a street sign. The flailing rope tied around his neck flew out and wrapped around the pole, yanking him to a dead stop.

Whew. Close call. Alarmingly close.

Coincidence? I think not.

My friend Esther was heartbroken that there was no family photo of her husband and herself with their son (their only living child) and new daughter-in-law at their wedding. Somehow the photographer had neglected to take a shot of the four of them as he'd assembled various family members for pictures.

Esther had repeatedly sorted through all the candid pictures that had been taken with their personal cameras and asked everyone she knew who had snapped photos at the wedding to look through theirs. Sadly, no family portrait ever showed up.

Still, Esther prayed. That special, intimate depiction of the occasion was her heart's desire.

Three years later, Esther was looking for a particular photo and was going through hundreds of shots from her camera that had been transferred to a flash drive. Wonder of wonders, there appeared a perfect image of Esther and her husband, son, and daughter-in-law together at the wedding. It was a picture she'd never seen before. And she had seen them all.

Where did it come from? It seemed to have just appeared out of nowhere.

Happenstance? No way. The framed eight-by-ten glossy now resides in an honored spot on Esther's credenza as a reminder of the Almighty's amazing grace.

ROCKIN' TO THE BEAT

Grace notes—that's what I call these special little touches from Papa God that remind us that the details of our lives are important to Him. That He's always watching. That He's got our back.

I borrowed the term from my twenty years as a piano teacher. Grace notes, as you probably know, are teensy musical notes added to regular notes that aren't essential to the melody but add breadth and depth and beauty to the music. Grace notes are a lovely bit of occasional flourish that aren't necessary for maintaining musical integrity but are an exquisite addendum that augment the score in delightfully surprising ways.

That's what Papa's grace notes do for us. They're His fingerprints. . .everyday mini-miracles. . .little silvery tones of grace that indelibly imprint His love on our lives. Grace notes are physical demonstrations of His (agape) love for us.

The trouble is that we get so wrapped up in the bustling busyness of everyday living, we often miss the grace notes. Their sweet consonance just floats right past our spiritual ears and out the bathroom window. But we need to hear those grace notes, sister, so we can twirl and dance and get our bad selves down to the internal music with which our Creator underscores our lives.

Like the sound track to a movie, music makes or breaks the entire experience.

I mean really, what would that famous scene in *Chariots of Fire* be without the awesome, bone-resonating music driving it? Just a dude in his boxers running on a beach.

Or how silly would Rocky Balboa have looked—a sweaty guy in a nondescript sweatshirt pumping his fists in the air at the top of a huge pile of steps in Philly—without that familiar triumphant beating strain, "Da-da-daaaaa, da-da-daaaaa," playing behind him?

If you're like me, you can't even hear two measures of *The Notebook* theme song without bursting into sobs. That's how powerful music can be.

I don't know about you, but on Judgment Day, I want my life's movie sound track to be filled with moments of big, booming tympani, happy flute trills, rip-up-the-keyboard boogie-woogie piano solos, and majestic string masterpieces. With a beat box and lots of cello thrown in. And an entire Beethoven symphony bedazzled with grace notes.

A MIND IS A TERRIBLE THING TO LOSE

Okay, I just have to tell you about a grace note that made me laugh. Papa has such a wicked sense of humor.

After my daughter's wedding, quite a few decorations turned up missing. I didn't have a clue what happened to them, and these were items she'd promised to a good friend, another bride-to-be, for her upcoming wedding. I felt terrible since sorting out the nuptial aftermath had been entrusted to me while Cricket happily honeymooned. The worrisome items were nowhere to be found, and the friend's wedding was rapidly approaching.

Knowing no problem is too trivial for our Protector and Provider—even AWOL wedding froofra—I prayed about it. "Instead of worrying, pray" (Philippians 4:6 MSG). What in the world had happened to all that stuff? It was too bulky for me to have misplaced or stuffed under a bed. Nevertheless we searched every nook and cranny. Nope. Nothing.

So there we were, Cricket and I, sitting in the splendor of yet another wedding a few weeks after hers (seemed like everybody she knew got married that year) when I started glancing around. Hmm. Things began to look suspiciously familiar. I poked Cricket in the ribs. "Say, aren't those your tulle bows on the pews?" I whispered incredulously. "And the silk flowers on the altar? And look, there's the missing garland, too!"

It turns out that in a gush of generosity, I'd told the MOB (who was an immense help with Cricket's wedding) that she could borrow anything she wanted. Then in the frenzy of the cleanup, I promptly forgot all about it and didn't notice her lugging the loot home after the wedding.

My daughter was ready to deck me right in the middle of the I dos.

I could only roll my eyes heavenward and mutter, "Thank You, Lord. Glad Your memory is better than mine."

MIRACLE MEMORY

Speaking of memory, this would be a good time to chat about an outstanding way to recognize and remember Papa's grace notes: miracle memory. I introduced the concept in *Fear, Faith, and a Fistful of Chocolate* and have heard that many women are now using this simple system to stay connected with their heavenly Father through greater awareness of His sometimes-overlooked work in our lives.

You know how muscle memory works? That, of course, is how limber little gymnasts learn to land a back tuck on a four-inch beam and what enables baseball pitchers to hit the inside corner of the plate without beaning the batter.

After I'd botched yet another arpeggio, my ancient piano teacher used to say, "Practice makes perfect, Debora," and you know, she was right. Lack of practice is self-evident in our myriad mistakes and poor confidence, but by doing the same thing over and over, our muscles learn to reflexively react a certain way. That's how pianists play a twelve-page sonata by memory. We don't have to think it through the tenth or the thirtieth or the hundredth time—our muscles automatically default to what they've learned through repetition. And our confidence in the outcome grows alongside our skill level.

Muscle memory.

Faith works the same way. When Papa God repeatedly works His everyday miracles (grace notes) in our lives, we develop *miracle* memory. Then we can automatically default to knowing He loves us and is still in control during those times when trials try to tell us otherwise.

And a good way to hasten that default to faith is to keep track of those everyday miracles in a prayer journal—a little flip pad you carry in your purse or car (I have one in both). Use your prayer pad to jot down your grace notes and prayer requests, big and small. Of course electronic versions work equally as well. Then be sure to record His answers to your prayers. Now you've got Papa's track record right in front of you; solid evidence that He has in the past, is currently in the present, and will in the future continue to care intimately about the details of your life.

Proof of His presence is right there in black and white, and you can take it to the bank. And our confidence in the outcome grows alongside our faith level.

Prayer pads are really quite therapeutic. When you're beginning to freak during a marathon wait at the dentist's office, or when you're stuck in maddening traffic and some bald guy in a red Ferrari cuts you off, whip out your prayer pad and start prayer-tweeting. You will not believe how fast your sky-high grumplitude barometer drops and your temp normalizes when you're conversing with the Guy who made the weather.

It's a surefire way to replace road rage with prayer and praise in your rolling cathedral (your new herspective of your car). Hey, we can be whelmed by life without being overwhelmed.

Papa God will listen to you: "Call to me and I will answer you," (Jeremiah 33:3 NIV)—and He'll work behind the scenes on your behalf with a big loving smile on His face. As popular author and minister Max Lucado says, "Love is about listening." And it absolutely is. Papa is ready and waiting to listen to us when nobody else will give us the time or attention.

We can depend on Him, girlfriend. We can rely on Him when people—even the best of people—let us down. "We know and rely on the love God has for us" (1 John 4:16 NIV). His love for us is as sure as a scorched tongue in a chili cook-off.

While Chuck and I were in Italy on our anniversary trip, our tour guide said a peculiar thing. While referring to the miraculous survival of people in a horrific volcanic eruption (not Pompeii, a different eruption), she said in her heavy Italian accent, "It's not important to us (the inhabitants of Naples) that we believe in miracles, only that we have them."

Think about that a minute. Many people see miracles and write them off as having nothing to do with a higher power. They're just coincidence. Or happenstance. Or luck. But I ask you: What sense is there in acknowledging miracles without acknowledging the Miracle-Maker?

THE FIFTY-SIXTH CAKE

Okay, at the risk of my editor stringing me up by my earlobes because this chapter is getting too long, I must include just one more grace note (I declare, I could keep talking about grace notes all day!). This one will give you God-bumps.

Not long ago it was my privilege to speak to a large gathering of women celebrating chocolate (what could possibly be more celebratory?). The church hosting the event had been advertising and selling tickets for nearly six weeks. Many, many prayers had been lifted up asking the Lord to bless this community outreach event honoring Him. A week prior to the event, four hundred tickets had been sold, and fifty fancy chocolate layer cakes were ordered from a local bakery to serve as the centerpieces of each round table and dessert for the ladies sitting there.

These were not just your run-of-the-mill chocolate cakes; they were culinary masterpieces, adorned with chocolate curls and doodads and ornate decorations that with a mere glance would make your saliva spray like a fireman's hose.

During the two days just before the celebration, a rush of ticket orders came in, and the good ladies just couldn't bring themselves to turn anyone away. Another five cakes were rush ordered and scheduled to be picked up right before the program started.

As the designated cake-picker-upper drove to the bakery on the afternoon of the event, she received a frantic call from the church. Ten more last-minute tickets had been purchased. There were nearly five hundred now coming. Another table would be added. Another cake would be needed.

"But there's no way they can make another cake that fast," she told the caller. "And those fifty-five cakes were custom decorated just for us. I'll look to see what they've got already made but we may have to just get a plain one. . .if they have any at all. Pray hard."

As she waited for the preordered cakes to be boxed, she saw that there were no additional chocolate cakes in the display case. She lamented to the lady in the hairnet that she really, *really* needed another cake. Was there anything they could possibly do?

A big smile spread across the white-aproned lady's face. "I'm the baker," she said. "I have a surprise for you." She disappeared into the back room and reappeared holding another beautifully decorated chocolate cake exactly like the other fifty-five.

"Something told me I should make an extra cake," she said with a grace note twinkle in her eye. Or maybe Someone.

Miracles are like pimples, because once you start looking for them you find more than you ever dreamed you'd see.

~Daniel Handler, alias Lemony Snicket

FOLLOWING MY PERSONAL GPS (GOD-POWERED SATELLITE)

1. C. S. Lewis said, "Miracles are a retelling of the very same story which is written across the whole world in letters too large for some of us to see." Tell about an everyday miracle (grace note) that showed you that Papa God cares about the tiniest details of your life.

2. What type of music or specific songs would be playing on the sound track of a movie about your life?

3. How clear is your miracle memory? Do you have a system for keeping track of Papa God's track record in your life? If not, how about putting some thought into developing one?

4. Go back and reread Psalm 18:24 (at the beginning of this chapter). What does this verse mean to you in light of recognizing that everyday miracles aren't just coincidence or luck?

5. Take another look at 1 John 4:16 just before the fifty-sixth cake story. In what ways do you know and rely on Papa's love for you?

CHAPTER 10

Who's Driving This Bus?
(Developing Trust)

---

*Trust in the LORD with all your heart;
do not depend on your own understanding.
Seek his will in all you do, and he
will show you which path to take.*
PROVERBS 3:5–6 NLT

My friend Marianne was sweating out her options. Her husband had died unexpectedly less than a year before, and finances were so tight, she wasn't sure she'd be able to keep her home. A long-time believer, Marianne had always trusted God to take care of her, and He always had. But this time, things looked pretty grim. She needed to find a boarder ASAP to share expenses. Unfortunately, she had lost most of her eyesight to macular degeneration and couldn't drive, so the only work she could find was part-time babysitting in her home, which didn't provide enough pennies to stretch.

She hadn't been able to buy new clothes in years and only owned two bras, both purchased so long ago that their elastic had given up the ghost. Her panties were just as raggedly pathetic, but even WalMart underwear was an expense she couldn't justify when keeping a roof over her head was top priority.

So Marianne prayed. But she couldn't help wondering if Papa

God truly cared about minutia like Fruit-of-the-Loom. I mean, really, when there were famines to resolve, wars to prevent, and diseases to heal, what was a saggy bosom and droopy drawers?

But she soon found out how very much He cared.

Out of the blue, an acquaintance called asking if Marianne happened to need any clothes. They were in good shape, she said, but she just needed to clean out her overstuffed closet and bulging bureau. She admitted to having a bit of a. . .well, shopping. . . um, *affinity*. It was time again to purge and start over. If Marianne didn't want the items, they were headed to the thrift shop.

"Well, sure!" Marianne replied and almost busted a gut when the woman brought over twenty-seven bras, fifty-seven pairs of panties, plus huge piles of blouses and pants that all fit perfectly. They were excellent quality—much better than Marianne could have possibly afforded, even buying them piece by piece.

Thank goodness one woman's addiction is another woman's addition.

As if that weren't enough of a miracle, Marianne then received a call from a widow she'd never met looking for a room to rent. It, too, was a perfect fit.

As we discovered in the last chapter, recognizing the source of everyday miracles is essential to developing trust. But sometimes trust is hard to come by, especially when a chunk of time goes by without recognizing a single grace note and life feels like a big ol' driverless bus careening out of control. But those are the times when the King of glory does His best work—when our lives become a testimony to His unfailing love.

It's been said that testimony is the result of a test with a lot of moaning. What's really in our heart is revealed during crises. Do we trust God enough to put our lives in His hands?

TRUST IS RISKY BUSINESS

In the book of Genesis, Abraham was asked to do the unthinkable: sacrifice his only son, Isaac. To literally put his precious boy's life in God's hands—the sweet, happy child God had blessed him with in his old age. Can you imagine the terrible struggle he went through in deciding whether to obey the Ancient of Days or grab his boy and haul patootie? I hate to think what I might have done. But Abraham chose to trust God, although he couldn't see any possible solution. The Lord, however, with His famous thirteenth-hour timing, provided the solution and took Abraham's faith to the next level in the process. "Abraham called the name of that place The Lord Will Provide" (Genesis 22:14 NASB).

That's one of God's names in Hebrew, you know—Jehovah Jireh, which is translated, "Our Provider." And provide for us He does. Despite our anemic trust.

I love watching my toddler grandbuddy Blaine learning trust. He stands on the pool's edge and sees his daddy standing a few feet away in water Blaine knows is scary deep, holding out big, strong arms and telling him to jump. At first Blaine backs away, frightened, unable to translate what he knows about his daddy into action—that he loves him passionately and would never lead him to harm. It takes awhile, and Blaine waffles with the decision about whether to trust his dad to the point of surrendering control.

Inch to the edge, back off. Inch to the edge, back off.

It's a hard thing giving up control, isn't it? You and I know that all too well.

But Blaine finally does, and a whole new world opens up for him. Once Blaine takes the leap of faith and realizes that his papa is completely trustworthy, only then is he ready to go to the next level of trust: facing the roaring garbage truck monster without running to hide under the bed. And then the ultimate: learning to ride a two-wheeler.

That's the way we develop trust, too. Once we take the leap of faith in giving up control, we're able to translate what we know about Papa God into action—that He loves us passionately and would never lead us to harm. I've referred to this verse already, but it's far too awesome not to repeat: "Never will I leave you; never will I forsake you" (Hebrews 13:5 NIV).

TRUST MELTDOWN

That Hebrews verse is especially meaningful to me because of a parenting error I made when my daughter was young. Sure, we all make mistakes in raising our kids, but this one was huge, and I still cringe over it twenty years later.

My daughter Cricket was seven years old at the time and had been having a hard time with separation anxiety. She'd had trouble letting me out of her sight since infancy, but she'd been exceptionally clingy that summer and I was exhausted and more than ready for an adult time-out.

We were on our annual Daytona Beach vacation with my parents and sister's family, and our two kids were having a blast playing with their cousins. When Chuck and I learned we'd need to leave three days early to take care of something at home, my parents and sister offered to keep the kids and return them to our house at week's end.

Well, to me the prospect of three whole days of grown-up time sounded like paradise. A no-brainer. We knew our son would be fine with it, but the problem was how to get away without Cricket having a meltdown and ruining our plans.

It was at that point that I made one of the worst decisions of my life. The solution seemed simple: we'd just disappear. We wouldn't tell her we were going. So we covertly packed our bags and snuck them into the car. Then when Cricket and her cousin went into a back room to play, we quietly crept out without telling her good-bye.

Ah, such freedom! We turned off our phones to avoid the on-slaught of calls we knew would be coming and were almost giddy with relief on the three-hour drive home. It wasn't until we walked into the too-quiet house and I was confronted with Cricket's be-loved teddy bear lying forlornly on the couch that I started to feel the full impact of what I'd done. I had abandoned my daughter. I'd left her and forsaken her without explanation. Without any assurance of my love. She'd trusted me, and I had disregarded her needs and thought only of my own.

I had no doubt I was the worst parent ever.

The next three days were a blur of tearful phone calls and reports from my parents of a very sad little girl sitting by herself mourning in silence while the other children played and laughed and swam. She wouldn't eat and cried herself to sleep. She was too young and immature to understand why we'd left and felt only the painful breach of trust in the two people she'd trusted most. Her little world crumbled.

I'm sorry to say it took a long time before that trust was restored.

JUST SHOW UP WITH A
TEASPOON OF WILLINGNESS

Trust is a sacred thing. Papa God's Hebrews 13:5 promise (which is actually a recap of Deuteronomy 31:8) is incredibly significant. When He says He'll *never* leave or forsake us, that's powerful, sister. *Never*. Not ever will we be abandoned. Oh, we may feel abandoned at times, like Cricket did, but the truth is that we are never truly abandoned by our heavenly parent, who loves us with far more pure, sweet, righteous love than any earthly parent ever could.

My writer bud Rhonda Rhea addresses those fleeting feelings of desolation so well: "Never judge God's love for you by your circumstances. Pain and tragedy that interrupt life are not proof that He's not caring. His love for you is immensely bigger than the pain you're carrying."

On days when we're out of sync with Papa's limitless love, when we're feeling deserted, forsaken, or betrayed, we have to remember that feelings aren't trustworthy. These are the times to overrule our hearts with our heads. These are the times when we just need to show up with a teaspoon of willingness and wait to see what the one who wants only the best for us will do.

Sure, it would be nice to possess a cavernous vat of trust we could dip into on bad days, but really, who has that? Not me. Not you. The good news is that all we really need is a teaspoon of willingness and to show up. Papa God will do the rest.

For Christ-followers, showing up is half the battle. Willingness is what matters. Even if it's only a teaspoonful. Like Blaine at the pool, we choose to believe. We choose trust. So we finally jump. And Papa God catches us in His big, strong arms, and we begin to feel the love that was there all along. Yes, Jehovah Jireh, Our Provider, truly does provide for us. Often in unexpected ways.

A PAPA WHO PROVIDES

My friend Frances was asked by her neighbors to take care of their dog while they were away on vacation. For the first few days, Frances faithfully walked next door to feed and walk the dog. But then one afternoon the neighbor's house key went missing. Frances searched the entire area around the hook where she'd always hung the key and everywhere else she could think of as day turned to night. She began to panic, picturing that poor starving dog staring dejectedly at the door waiting for her arrival. He would be a skeleton by the time her neighbors returned if she didn't find that key.

Frances was stumped. Should she break a window? Jimmy the lock? Call the fire department?

Instead Frances prayed in earnest, "Lord, You're the God who sees. Please show me where that key is." And she suddenly had a flashback of carrying the overflowing laundry basket right by the key hook. Now that was the one place she hadn't looked. Sure enough, she found the key buried deep within her daughter's clean clothes in the laundry basket in her room. If her daughter was true to form, those clothes wouldn't have been folded for a week.

Papa provided.

My friend Gloria didn't know what to do. Her daughter Elizabeth had worked hard all the way through college to her final semester, but funds had dried up. Gloria had no way to pay for Elizabeth's last three classes. She'd exhausted even the remotest possibilities she could muster on her own power, so she leaned on her trust in Papa God. She prayed, believing He would somehow provide the answer.

Gloria felt compelled to contact the business department at Elizabeth's college, although she knew it was way too late to apply for financial assistance for the upcoming semester. It so happened that the man she spoke with on the phone was the same little boy that Gloria had helped get through his six-year-old sister's death when she'd taught him in fourth grade decades before. Gloria had done everything she could that school year to reach out to Mark in his confusion and grief and make him feel special and loved, even taking him out to dinner and on after-school outings to play basketball or video games with other children.

And he hadn't forgotten.

When Gloria explained her situation and need for assistance, Mark became very quiet. He then promised a return call the following day.

True to his word, when Mark phoned, he said in a tear-choked voice, "Miss Gloria, you helped me through the loss of my little sister not only as a teacher, but as a friend; I just had to find a way to help you." Mark had personally gone to the financial aid department and arranged for Elizabeth's $2,000 tuition to be covered, all except for $80.

When we face what seems like insurmountable mountains, small, everyday speed humps, or even elastic-challenged droopy drawers, if we simply show up with our teaspoon of willingness to seek Papa God's will, He truly will catch us when we jump. He'll turn our mess into His message.

Yep. In God we trust; all others we screen calls.

Trust means not asking for the Almighty's references.
~DEBORA M. COTY

FOLLOWING MY PERSONAL GPS (GOD-POWERED SATELLITE)

1. What was your favorite story of trust in this chapter and why?

2. What is your favorite personal story of trust in your life or someone you're close to?

3. Can you recall a time in your life when you lost trust in someone? Was that trust ever restored? If so, what did it take to restore it? If not, why was it unsalvageable?

4. Do you find it hard to inch to the edge of the pool and jump into Papa God's waiting arms? Why or why not?

5. Was there ever a time when you lost trust in the Lord? Some days trust feels as distant as Mars. Just showing up with a teaspoon of willingness is the least and the most we can do. How about you? What's currently happening in your life for which you need to rustle up a teaspoonful?

CHAPTER 11

Jiggle the Thingie and Keep on Cranking
(Spending Time in Papa God's Waiting Room)

Wait on the Lord; be of good courage,
and He shall strengthen your heart.

PSALM 27:14 NKJV

My silver-haired friend RC pulled into a convenience store one day to get some change. As he opened his door, he noticed a car coasting to a stop about five yards downhill from the gas pump. Apparently it couldn't quite make the finish line on its remnant fumes.

The driver got out of the car, wrung his hands, and then noticed RC standing there. "Do you think you could give me a hand here, buddy?" the guy asked. "Just need a little push."

"Sure," RC said, happy to exercise both his muscles and his Christianity. As he placed his hands on the trunk and assumed the "get ready" position, he was dumbfounded to see the driver climb back in the nice warm car beside his passenger, close the door, and grip the steering wheel, waiting expectantly for a complete stranger to single-handedly shove his two-ton vehicle up the hill.

RC, being the big-hearted fellow he is, instead of throwing his hands in the air and walking away, sauntered over to the clueless guy's window and quipped, "Sir, I realize you might have confused me for the Incredible Bulk, but I really can't push this car without your help."

I had to laugh when RC told me this story because it sounds so much like something I might do in my zeal to accomplish a task—expect the one going out of his way, helping me out of the kindness of his heart, to do all the heavy work. And do it *now*. Uh-huh. I'll steer, you push. Sounds like me. And maybe you, too.

More often than not, that kind someone helping us is Papa God, and He's not opposed to doing the hardest part. . .as long as we do all we can and then trust Him to take over and do what only He can.

KICKING BETWEEN THE GOAL POSTS

Doing all we can usually involves setting and working toward goals. Striving to achieve a specific objective keeps our head in the game and motivates us to persevere. Goals are steps on the stair-case of life; we've gotta have them to keep inching upward or we can stall out and end up floundering in the quagmire. Wallowing in the muck. Drowning in the stress-pool.

Establishing goals—both short- and long-term goals—ensures we make it to our desired final destination in this life. (You can find more about goal-setting in the "Playing Chicken with a Duck" chapter in my book *More Beauty, Less Beast*.) Hey, I'm not just talking about jobs, social status, or athletic achievement here. We need goals to acquire important personal qualities. . .spiritual qualities we care deeply about, like becoming more Christlike, more patient, more loving.

Speaking of becoming more patient, I saw a bumper sticker that said, "Patience is the ability to count down before you blast off." A worthy goal indeed. I think I'll have that etched onto my rearview mirror.

I have a poster on the door of my writing cave (that's what my daughter calls my office) that states my long-term love goals. I look at them every day. In fact, I'm looking at them right now. They're directly from 1 Corinthians 13, "The love chapter":

> *Love is patient, love is kind.*
> *It does not envy, it does not boast,*
> *It is not proud.*
> *It is does not dishonor others, it is not self-seeking,*
> *It is not easily angered,*
> *It keeps no record of wrongs.*
> *Love does not delight in evil*
> *But rejoices with the truth.*
> *It always protects, always trusts,*
> *Always hopes, always perseveres.*
> *Love never fails.* (verses 4–8 NIV)

This passage describes how profoundly the Lover of our souls loves us and sets the bar for how we should love others. I'm not there yet (especially the goals in the first, fifth, and sixth lines), but I like to think I'm making progress. Okay, s-l-o-w progress.

Sure, I have goals and you do, too, even if you haven't given it much thought. Physical goals are easier to assess. You have a to-do list, right? Case closed. Goals are the means by which to succeed in whatever we hope to accomplish before we lay our weary bodies down for that final dirt nap.

Goals we accomplish—or leave dangling like chads in Florida—can follow us to the grave.

You know, I'm no procrastinator, but I do tend to put things off that I don't like to do. . .which might turn out to be embarrassing one day. When I hop the great spiritual divide and am rejoicing with Jesus in my new afterlife celestial digs, I'd really rather not have folks down on earth discover my piles of undone to-do lists, unfinished projects, and halfhearted attempts at housecleaning. So I penned a little ditty I call. . .

> The Procrastinator's Prayer
> *If I die before daybreak,*
> *I pray the Lord sends someone great*
> *To hide the mess I made too late*
> *And scrub my stove before the wake.*

Conversely, there are those Superwoman days (no doubt caused by schizophrenic hormones—I blame everything on hormones, or lately the lack thereof) when we decide that we simply must conquer all of our lifetime goals *today*. That unrealistic pressure we put on ourselves is exactly what leads me to chant. . .

> The Overachiever's Get-Over-It Creed
>   (based on Philippians 4:13)
> *"I can do all things through Christ"*
> *does NOT mean*
> *I will do all things,*
> *all at once,*
> *all by myself,*
> *all before the sun goes down.*

In other words, overachievers need to engage in the three Ps: prioritize, plan, and pace yourself. Papa puts only enough fuel in your tank each day to arrive safely at the destination He has routed out for you. All the extra detours you tack on will either run you out of gas or land you in a ditch.

SOLVING THE FRUSTRATION EQUATION

So what happens when we can't reach our goals? When we're blocked by forces beyond our control and end up bedraggled, frustrated, and draped across a plaid armchair in Papa God's waiting room?

We all know how maddening it is to be stuck in a doctor's office waiting room for hours on end (thank heavens for e-readers!). But how do we handle long stints waiting for significant life events to finally occur? For our prayers to be answered? For Papa God to move?

My frustration equation for extended time in Papa God's waiting room goes like this: Humor + Faith + Perseverance = Survival. Honestly, it's the only answer to making it through those long periods of purgatorial lag time without ripping your mustache out follicle by agonizing follicle. (I call that unfortunate menopausal symptom the Clark Gable phenomenon.)

In this microwavable, instant gratification, nanosecond connection era in which we live, we rue waiting. And our contention regarding physical waiting oozes over into our spiritual life; we resist waiting on the Lord, too. Especially when it requires continued effort and perseverance. Yet it's inevitable. We'll all do time in Papa's God's waiting room. So it would behoove us to learn how to gracefully endure.

My friend Pati is learning to wait on the Lord in a way she never expected. Pati is a Christ-follower. Her husband, Cliff, although an upstanding, moral man, is not.

Pati, whose intimate relationship with the Lord began shortly after her marriage to Cliff, yearns more than anything for her husband to become part of the family of God through saving faith in Jesus Christ. It's her heart's desire, her greatest goal, for her husband to spend eternity with Pati and their son in heaven.

So for the past decade Pati has been bombarding Cliff with praise music, taped sermons, invitations to every imaginable church event, and overtly evangelical books. She argues, she cajoles, she sweetly pleads. . .to the point of, well, nagging. Pati is so intent to "win him over" she forgets that the Lord's perfect timing isn't always ours.

One evening after dinner when Pati was revving up her sales pitch, she noticed her five-year-old son, Branden, standing in the hallway beckoning her with one waggling finger. Branden, a devoted and wise-beyond-his-years believer since he was barely out of diapers, led Pati to a spot out of Cliff's earshot. I daresay that boy must've been filled with the Spirit in utero like John the Baptist! (Did you know that cool snippet of trivia about Jesus' cousin? It's found in Luke 1:15. Okay, back to the story.)

"Mom," Branden said, looking earnestly up into her eyes. "Do you know what the symbol for the Holy Spirit is?"

Flustered by her inability to reach Cliff, coupled with her son's seemingly off-the-wall question, Pati answered in hand-on-hip snarky flair, "No, Branden. What is it?"

"A dove," Branden said quietly. "It's a dove, Mom. Not a woodpecker."

Yo. Out of the mouth of babes (although I think that child was born thirty and should have been named Solomon. Or Yoda. Or both.).

So now whenever Pati, in her impatience, pushes Cliff too hard, Branden makes a silent woodpecking gesture with his hand, and Pati is reminded that from Jehovah's perspective, "Just as the heavens are higher than the earth, so are my ways higher than your ways and my thoughts higher than your thoughts" (Isaiah 55:9 NLT).

It's not up to Pati to save Cliff. That's Papa's job. In Papa's time. Pati's job is to do all she can to love Cliff and live a life honoring Christ, trusting Papa to take over and do what only He can do.

WORTH THE WAIT

As Pati has discovered, waiting is never easy. Waiting and endurance—two sides of the same character-building coin. Romans 5:4–5 (CEV) declares, "Endurance builds character, which gives us a hope that will never disappoint us." The Greek word for character here is *charakter*, which, according to Webster, pertains to the mark made by an engraving tool or chisel. As author Jane Kirkpatrick astutely observes, "It's the obstacles in life that carve out character. That's what's left over after you've been gouged out."

And hope, the byproduct produced by all that gouging and chiseling in Papa God's waiting room, will never disappoint us. Because that hope is begotten by love—the greatest, deepest, most fathomless love that exists. It will never, ever fail us. "God will never let you down" (1 Corinthians 10:13 MSG).

It's Papa God's bottomless love that stands beside us through financial hardship, failing health, and rocky relationships. It's His relentless love that carries us when we're exhausted, emboldens us when we're timid, and comforts us when we're afraid. It's the love so incredibly deep that even though we're enamored with sin and don't deserve a second chance, Papa gives us one anyway. "God demonstrates His own love toward us, in that while we were yet sinners, Christ died for us" (Romans 5:8 NASB).

So dear sister, are you pacing Papa God's waiting room waiting. . .waiting. . .waiting? Wondering when your wait will end. . . your wounds will mend. . .your future will begin? Are you tired of pushing the two-ton car uphill and fresh out of goals?

Listen to me: Clutch the blanket of hope around you and believe with all your heart that although Papa's seldom early, He's never late.

I understand, I really do. I'm pacing right behind you.

One of my favorite scriptures during emotionally taxing

seasons in Papa's waiting room has always been Isaiah 40:31: "Those who trust in the LORD will find new strength. They will soar high on wings like eagles. They will run and not grow weary. They will walk and not faint" (NLT).

How can anyone *not* be uplifted by that passage? It's bursting with promise—the promise that waiting will not weaken but empower us; that our own personal Superhero will infuse us with His supernatural strength so that spiritually we can hang glide from mountaintops, outrun locomotives, and power walk to the ends of the earth hand in hand with our loving Papa.

Now that's worth the wait, don't you think?

A handful of patience is worth more than a bushel of brains.
~DUTCH PROVERB

⊘ FOLLOWING MY PERSONAL GPS
(GOD-POWERED SATELLITE)

1. Which do you need more often, the Procrastinator's Prayer or the Overachiever's Get-Over-It Creed? Or are you like me and need both, depending on which direction the hormones are blowing that day?

2. What three life goals are your main focus during the season of life you're in right now?

3. What is your usual response when achievement of a goal is blocked? Anger? Acceptance? Resentment? Frustration? Now would be a good time to review the frustration equation; are there any components of the equation you may need to beef up for the next time you're in survival mode—humor, faith, perseverance?

4. How do you cope when you find yourself pacing Papa God's waiting room? When was the last time you were there? For what were you waiting?

5. It's very important for us to review Papa's past faithfulness during our waiting room time. Deuteronomy 4:9 is a good reminder: "You must be very careful not to forget the things you have seen God do for you. Keep reminding yourselves, and tell your children and grandchildren as well" (CEV).

CHAPTER 12

Oh Me of Little Faith
(Embracing Limitless Love)

My purpose is to give them a rich and satisfying life.
JOHN 10:10 NLT

I once knew a boy. He was a blond-haired, creamy-milk-chocolate-eyed boy with a sunny smile. I liked that boy very much. On my first day of school, as I wept my six-year-old heart out and clung to my daddy's leg, begging him not to leave me all alone, that little blond boy smiled at me.

I didn't feel so afraid anymore. I had a friend.

Randy continued to be my friend throughout elementary and middle school. In our small town, we were thrown together in the same classes at school almost every year and even sang in the youth choir at the same church. Randy was smart, cute, and quick with a contagious grin. He had a carefree, easygoing way about him that was totally cool. Kind of like the Deep South take on a surfer dude. He was polite and popular and well-liked by kids and adults alike. I must admit that I "angsted" my way through unrequited adolescent crushes on him more than once.

But then one day in high school, that sweet blond boy who had smiled at me on the first day of school disappeared. In his place appeared a painfully thin, hollow-eyed stranger who didn't seem to care about much. Rumors involving drugs and alcohol flew as Randy began to hang out with the party crowd.

At the time, I was unaware that Randy had experienced upheaval at home as his parents divorced and his mother remarried. Randy had decided on divorce, too; he opted to divorce himself. That meant turning his back on the things that had mattered to him most. . .friends, family, and faith.

Looking back at that tumultuous time in his life, Randy now says, "As a young teen, I thought the difference between right and wrong was very clear. I believed in God and knew all about Jesus. But what I didn't have was a relationship. God was tugging on my heart, but I rejected His calling. I was crushed by my parents' divorce. Getting high seemed to make the hard things in my life easier. Drugs and alcohol became my best friends."

By age twenty-five, Randy had dropped out of college and become a daily user of alcohol, pot, and often cocaine. He had morphed into a master of subterfuge and managed to hide his addictions despite his job as a heavy machine operator. "I often drove vehicles drunk, broke many laws, and had no respect for myself, much less others."

Then one horrible day Randy's uncle, with whom he was very close, was murdered by his own wife. Randy was subpoenaed to testify about his knowledge of their relationship, and there he met Kim, a friend of Randy's uncle, also called to testify.

Unexpected romance blossomed between Randy and Kim and grew over several years before they eventually married. But Randy continued to live in secret addiction. Eight years later, Randy found himself without a job, with a marriage on the rocks, and with self-esteem so low that he refused to stand in front of a mirror to shave. He couldn't stand the sight of himself and hated the man he had become. He wanted out. But the iron grip of addiction held him prisoner.

Yet he still denied the truth. When Kim accused him of being an alcoholic, Randy angrily replied that he could stop drinking whenever he wanted, so he set out to prove her wrong. By sheer bullheaded willpower, he didn't have one drink for nine months. He'd proven his point. Right?

Wrong. One beer—just one small slip in a weak moment—sent him spiraling downward into even deeper addiction. For the next two years, Randy drank day and night. Instead of proving he wasn't an alcoholic, he'd proven he was. He couldn't break free on his own feeble, limited power. "I found that I couldn't live with alcohol," Randy admits, "nor live without it. That's a very bad place to be."

His relationship with his wife and children seemed irreparably broken. When Randy began wrestling with suicidal thoughts, as a last resort he turned to the thin thread of faith he'd carried with him since he had given his heart to Jesus at age nine. His desperate prayer was simple and direct: "God, please help me."

But would God recognize a voice He hadn't heard in many, many years? Someone who had intentionally turned away? Could the Creator of the entire universe possibly care that much about one stubborn, wayward bit of creation? Randy had his doubts.

LET'S MAKE A DEAL

Then the unbelievable happened. Randy heard the Almighty's answer as clearly as if He had spoken aloud: *"I will give you My strength. I'll do My part, but you must do yours."*

Randy wrapped his weary, discouraged heart around this undeserved hope for wholeness and embraced it. *Okay, Lord. It's a deal.*

To seal the deal publicly, Randy rededicated his life to Christ and was baptized. But even repented-of sin has repercussions.

Recovery was tough. Incredibly tough. After leaving the detoxi-fication center where he'd sobered up, Randy struggled to follow the twelve-step AA program and stay accountable. He had to learn not to drink one day at a time. But he found that the steps are spir-itual in nature and by diligently practicing those principles, his spir-itual and emotional, as well as his physical health slowly improved.

"Addiction affects the whole family," Randy concedes now. "The real problem is the thinking, not the drinking. Drinking is the symptom of a deeper problem. Self-centeredness and selfishness are the roots of addiction. I'd made a mess of things, and it took years to mend my life. Kim watched me suspiciously for a long time, expecting me to relapse. After all, I had promised to change for years; why should she trust me now?"

But trust she did, and Randy did, too—in the immense, un-fathomably deep, limitless power of Papa God.

Oh my goodness, you should see Randy and Kim now. The romantic chick in you would burst right into song. They act like newlyweds. Since Papa renewed their love and trust for each other as well as for Him, they're truly a couple again, heart and soul.

It's been twenty-one years since Randy took his last drink, and he's blazing a comeback trail for the Lord. Besides helping heal people physically at a hospital as a registered nurse, Randy helps many heal spiritually by sharing Jesus through a biker ministry (that's Suzuki, not Schwinn). He also visits prisons and jails to bring hope of a restored life to those battling addictions.

At our twenty-five-year high school reunion, Randy and I re-connected for the first time since we were eighteen. I'm pretty sure my mouth literally hung open. I absolutely could not believe the incredible change in him. His once-dead eyes are now alive and sparkling with the joy of living fully. Abundantly. Richly. His apa-thy has been replaced by excitement, his discouragement eclipsed by anticipation of what tomorrow will bring.

SPLISH SPLASH

Now really, sister, don't you want to live that way, too? To have a life so engorged with Papa's unconditional love that your joy and anticipation overflow like a pitcher that overfills a teacup and just keeps on pouring? I certainly do. One of the Life Savers on my calendar leaps to mind: "May the Master pour on the love so it fills your lives and splashes over on everyone around you" (1 Thessalonians 3:12 MSG).

I love the image projected by that word picture, don't you? Love so fulfilling and ample as it pours from Papa God's pitcher into our empty teacup selves that it overflows the brim and permeates the complete fiber of our lives. We become wringing, sloshing, wonderfully wet with His love and begin to splash on everyone around us.

You know, we don't have to have a history of addiction to be blown away by the magnitude of Papa God's limitless, no-matter-what-you've-done-I-love-you-anyway sentiment for us. We've all made mistakes, some that continue to haunt us with shame and heartache. Yes, we've all sinned and fallen w-a-y short of the person we wish we were. . .someone who reflects the glory of Papa God in all that we say, do, and think (my paraphrase of Romans 3:23).

But He knows none of us are perfect, and guess what? He's okay with that. He made us that way. We need Him to be whole. We're incomplete without Him. We just need to have faith that He will do what He said He will do if we ask, and deluge us with His saturating love.

Love that covers a multitude of sins (1 Peter 4:8).

Love that has enveloped us since we were a mere gleam in His eye; "We love Him because He first loved us" (1 John 4:19 NKJV).

Papa is standing by with his gigantic, bottomless love pitcher, ready to pour when're we're ready to receive.

Is your teacup open?

There must be a tomorrow, because my life overflows today.
~Lois Chartrand

FOLLOWING MY PERSONAL GPS (GOD-POWERED SATELLITE)

1. Have you ever done something that you were afraid was unforgivable? Something that built a wall between you and Papa God?

2. When did that wall get demolished? Or—be honest now— is it still there?

3. How important is the demolition of that dividing wall in your relationship with the Lord? How does the presence or absence of that wall relate to John 10:10 (at the beginning of this chapter)?

4. Randy was afraid that his poor choices and neglect of prayer would make him a complete stranger to God. Do you ever wonder if you speak to Papa enough for Him to recognize your voice?

5. Go back a few paragraphs and read 1 Thessalonians 3:12 aloud. How would you like for the Master's drippy, sloshy, sopping love to splash others in your life?

SECTION 3

Woohoo! Road Trip!

If we love each other, God lives in us,
and his love is truly in our hearts.
1 John 4:12 cev

CHAPTER 13

Backseat Driving
(Relinquishing Control)

To Him who is able to do exceedingly abundantly above all that we ask or think, according to the power that works in us, to Him be glory. . .forever and ever. Amen.
EPHESIANS 3:20–21 NKJV

The horrendous year was ebbing to a close. My friend Ellie and her husband, Stephen, both Christ-followers, were in a mess.

Stephen, age fifty, was out of work and had exhausted all known options. Ellie's energies were depleted from homeschooling their daughter, who'd been born with multiple handicaps.

Pressure was high, stress unbearable, relationships strained to the breaking point. Finances plummeted. Things were bad, really bad, with no end in sight. They knew Stephen's chances of finding another job at his age were slim. He'd done all he could do. The situation was completely out of their hands. They had reached the end of possible. Now they must depend on the Lord for the impossible.

And Papa delivered.

The first impossibility occurred when Stephen happened across an opening listed on the Internet for a high-level job in his field located in the city in which Ellie's only sister and her family lived two hours away. Recognizing that he was decidedly underqualified for this position and very likely wouldn't even get past the preliminary paper stage to a face-to-face interview, Stephen figured, "Well, what could it hurt to apply? It would be great to be near family; Ellie could sure use the support from her sister. Besides, things couldn't get any worse here."

Just before e-mailing in his application, Stephen dialed the company's general phone number to ask a question. The operator mistakenly patched him through to the unlisted cell number of the company's national personnel executive. . .the boss of the boss of the supervisor he should have been speaking to.

It shouldn't have ever happened.

Initially annoyed at the unauthorized interruption, "Who *are* you? How did you get this private number?" the upper management executive who answered gradually warmed up and entered into a pleasant conversation with Stephen. She ended up conducting an impromptu phone interview for the position. Superseding company protocol, she then instructed Stephen to send his application directly to her, bypassing the hundreds submitted via the website.

Half a dozen live interviews later (and one hundredfold that many prayers), Stephen got the job! Impossibility number one.

The next hurdle was selling their old house and finding a place to live in the new city that was workable for their daughter's special needs. It was a runaway seller's market, and houses were snatched up within hours of being listed. Every single house Ellie's sister (who was acting as their surrogate buyer) inquired about on their behalf had already been sold. She just missed dozens of homes, some by a matter of minutes.

Week after week, month after month, the search continued.

It became evident that the original plan—finding a house near family—was impossible. (There's that annoying word again!) The search spread into nearby towns. Still nothing.

Stephen, who was commuting to his new job four hours each

day, was running on fumes. But only physically. Spiritually, he and Ellie kept on praying and believing that Jehovah, who had obviously orchestrated this whole thing, was in control.

One day, without a single note of fanfare (don't you love how Papa rarely takes credit by blowing a trumpet when He moves?), Stephen and Ellie received an offer on their old house above their listing price. Then, 120 miles away, Ellie's sister hopped in her car to run an errand and happened upon a homeowner hammering a "For Sale by Owner" sign into the lawn of a lovely home just a few doors down from her own. She slammed on her brakes, deserted her car, and chased the surprised homeowner up the driveway.

What d'ya know? It was the perfect home in the perfect location. The only snafu? The price was well above Ellie and Stephen's budget. And by the end of that same day, another buyer was standing in line behind them offering the full asking price.

Time to ramp up prayer power to Helpcon 5.

Would you believe that the next afternoon the owners inexplicably agreed to drop the price $30k, right into the range Ellie and Stephen could afford? And get this: they threw in their big-screen TV free for Stephen and Ellie's visually impaired daughter. Impossibilities numbers two and three.

Now that's Papa answering prayer with flair!

Ready for yet another example of the wisdom in relinquishing the driver's seat to the best Driver?

TUG-OF-WAR OVER THE STEERING WHEEL

My friend Caryl struggled with giving up control when she was diagnosed with aggressive breast cancer at age forty-seven. She reluctantly boarded the breakneck emotional roller coaster, which sometimes carried her on a steady ascent to hope but then suddenly twisted, pitching her into steep chasms of disappointment and despair.

After a double mastectomy, she endured a year of chemo, which caused hair loss, pain, trembling hands, frequent injections in her stomach to boost white blood cells, arm swelling, insomnia, constant fatigue, and many other symptoms that ruthlessly assaulted her battered body.

Caryl felt angry that "everyone else's life kept on going while mine had been stopped in its tracks." She was helpless to change anything. But she had a choice: to keep fighting for control while fear and worry overtook her, or to trust God and turn the steering wheel over to Him.

Caryl chose trust. Psalm 46:10 became her life preserver in the turbulent waters: "Cease striving and know that I am God" (NASB). Cease striving. Only then will you *know* that I'm in control. In effect, the Lord was saying: "Stop. Hand it over to Me. I'll take care of you. You'll see."

"I was confident of only one thing," Caryl says looking back, "that God loved me. During the PET scan to see what the cancer was doing to my body, I was confident He was with me every step of the way. All I had was the Lord. I knew I could do nothing on my own to pass this test. He was my whole answer. It was up to Him, and whatever the results, He would be with me. He truly carried me through this most difficult time of my life. I called it my *God Fog*. He protected me in the midst of all the surgeries, chemo, and day-to-day problems. Faith gave me the courage to face each day with confidence and hope."

Of course, as you and I both know, breast cancer survivors continue to battle for many years. Caryl is still fighting. . .with spunk. "I have implants to make my chest look more normal. I have a hairpiece to help with my patchy baldness. Prior to my cancer diagnosis, I hated the idea of getting older. Now I understand that each birthday is a gift—one to be celebrated and enjoyed. I know God is in control, and I want my life to reflect His love and faithfulness to me."

You have friends like Caryl, too, don't you—courageous gals battling cancer? Maybe you're that courageous gal. If so, my heart goes out to you, sister, for we're all in this together. We support one another. We pray for one another. I would consider it a privilege to pray for you if you'll take a moment and drop me a line (my e-dress is on page 47). Why? Because you and I are women who are constantly learning to trust Papa God as we navigate unexplored rocky terrain. By joining hands we can help each other climb even the highest precipice.

Okay. Sniff. Time to lighten up. My mascara is smudging.

YOU FEED THEM

Thinking about Ephesians 3:20 at the beginning of this chapter reminds me of another time Jesus showed His signature panache in doing *exceeding abundantly beyond* what anyone believed was possible. The story is found in the ninth chapter of Luke.

Picture this: The twelve disciples were in quite a pickle. These devoted followers of Jesus, the select few, his inner-circle BFFs—the very guys who earlier in the same chapter Jesus Himself had given "power and authority to cast out demons and to heal all diseases"—couldn't figure out how to make lunch.

The band (so to speak) had just returned from their inaugural Heal the Masses tour, where they no doubt accumulated many admirers and a measure of fame. They'd performed miraculous feats of healing and power over the forces of darkness never before beheld by mortal man. Pretty amazing stuff.

No doubt it was a heady and exhilarating experience akin to

the debut of brand new rock stars today. Sort of like winning Israeli Idol.

So Peter, James, John, and their buds must have felt discombobulated and perhaps unjustly humbled to suddenly find themselves demoted from their newly acquired "Almost Famous" status to the lowly position of servants. Servants called upon to provide a meal in a barren desert for thousands upon thousands of teeming, dusty, hungry, getting-grumpier-by-the-minute people.

There was no Chick-fil-A behind the cactus hedge. Hungry Howie's didn't do wilderness delivery. The nearest town was miles away, and cash was tight.

So put yourself in Peter's sandals for a moment and imagine how you might have reacted to Jesus' simple but forthright directive: "You feed them."

I know what my reaction would be. "*AACK!* Who? Me? Feed five thousand men *plus* women and children? Are you *serious?* No way. That's absolutely impossible!"

Of course it was impossible. Ridiculous. Ludicrous.

In today's terms it would be like Justin Bieber being informed during intermission at his sold-out Madison Square Garden concert that a clause in his contract required him to roast wieners and make potato salad for the entire audience immediately following the show.

Maybe it's easier to relate to if you pretend you and your spouse have just arrived home from your son's big high school game to find a bazillion cars, two buses, and a dozen motorcycles piled in front of your house because Junior has invited his entire team and coaching staff plus cheerleaders and a few dozen fans over for homemade lasagna and your famous chocolate raspberry sponge cake.

Impossible. Ridiculous. Ludicrous. Yep—that was the exact point Jesus was making.

Your first emotional reaction to "You feed them," like Peter's and for sure mine, would likely have been panic. . .indignation. . . even anger to receive such a stern, blunt order. As if you're being tossed into tsunami floodwaters without a life jacket.

But I don't believe for one second that blunt or stern is the way Jesus meant it. Or even said it. Because it was tough love. He loved these guys vehemently, although He no doubt realized the diva dozen needed a little lesson in dependency after spreading their independent wings as healers on the hoof.

And maybe a fresh dose of humility, too.

IT'S SHOWTIME

In this SUV called life, we truly cannot drive from the backseat. We have zero visibility. Our arms are too short. And yet we keep straining, reaching, barking directions, and wrestling for control until we begin careening all over the road. After we hit the ditch a time or two, we finally realize we're completely dependent on the One in the driver's seat. The only possible way out of a seemingly impossible situation is through His power. And as He said to the apostle Paul in 2 Corinthians 12:9 (NLT), "My power works best in weakness."

So in this you-feed-the-ravenous-mob scenario with the disciples, it was time for the rubber to meet the road. Spit or swallow. In girl-speak, button up or put on a cami.

And Jesus, with a twinkle of amicable contention in His eye and a mischievous grin on His face, laid the faith challenge right out before them. *Hey, it's showtime, boys. YOU feed them.*

When we're faced with an impossible task, we must first come to the realization that we're totally sunk if our own power is the only resource available. Our own power is finite. It's flimsy. It's futile. It's an inflatable raft in a river of sharp rocks. We'll get absolutely nowhere until we climb in Jesus' dinghy and hand over the oar.

Well, you know the rest of the story. The boys in the band watched in amazement as the Master Provider multiplied a couple of fish sandwiches into enough food to feed a small city, leaving twelve baskets overflowing with leftovers.

Hey, Papa God's in the miracle business. He specializes in impossible, ridiculous, and ludicrous. If He tells you to feed a ravenous mob in a desert, He'll supply the sushi and breadsticks.

God grant me the serenity to accept the people I cannot change,
the courage to change the one I can, and the wisdom to know it's me.

~UNKNOWN

⊘ FOLLOWING MY PERSONAL GPS (GOD-POWERED SATELLITE)

1. Go back to the beginning of this chapter and read Ephesians 3:20–21 aloud. Are you really grasping the deeper meaning of those hope-spawning words? *Exceeding. Abundantly. Beyond.* Stop a moment and consider how they might apply to you.

2. When during the past year have you had a tug-of-war with Jehovah over the steering wheel of your life? Who won?

3. I love something Caryl said to me, "Take this as a warning: When you read scripture, it will change you if you apply it." Some of the passages that changed her life are Philippians 4:6–7, Luke 12:26, and Psalm 118:24 (look them up in your Bible). What's your go-to scripture for the times you're facing real trouble?

4. Do you sometimes feel that the outcome to your problems is entirely dependent on your own skills, problem-solving abilities, and strength? (Don't be afraid to admit it—most of us women do.) How does Psalm 46:10 (on page 119) apply to those times?

5. Can you remember when a hurdle you or someone close to you was facing seemed impossible. . .ridiculous. . .ludicrous? Were you able to let go and let God have the steering wheel? How did the situation play out?

CHAPTER 14

Paper or Plastic?
(Discernment)

———— ✳ ————

The wise in heart are called discerning.
PROVERBS 16:21 NIV

|||||||||||||||||||||||||||||||||||||||||||||||||||||||||||||||||||||||||||||||||||||||||||||||||||||||||||||

I could hardly believe my ears when I heard about the woman who was pulled over for running a red light and found to have a twenty-four pack of beer strapped securely in her passenger seat belt while a sixteen-month-old baby girl bounced around unrestricted in the backseat.

Poor choices. We all make them (but hopefully not as poor as that!). What to say; when to say or not say it. When to act; when to wait. Whether to be insistent or patient. What to wear; what to eat. And how much of both.

We ask ourselves: What would Jesus do?

What would my mother say?

What'll that hot guy think?

It's enough to frizz your bangs.

"Teach me good discernment," the psalmist implores Yahweh (God's ancient Hebrew name) in Psalm 119:66 (NASB). All of us attempting to please our heavenly Father in our minute-by-minute life decisions feel his angst.

As the psalmist knew, good discernment is an ongoing learning process; he prayed "teach me" in an active sense rather than "give me," in which the recipient is passive. We can't just sit around like a handful of linguini and wait for the holiness pot to boil and plump us up. In doing, we learn. Wisdom is borne of making mistakes. Someone wise once said, "Good decisions come from experience, and experience comes from bad decisions." Discernment is the mortar holding the bricks of our life decisions together.

But what exactly is good discernment?

It's the ability to analyze, understand, and judge from an enlightened perspective what is and is not from God. Thankfully, the Lord knew how confused we can get when we're so inundated with things not from God in the course of our every day. So He sent a Helper—the Holy Spirit—as our supernatural search engine to enable us to distinguish the difference.

The Holy Spirit specializes in helping us. . .guiding, revealing, discerning. Sorting the spiritual sugar from the arsenic. That's His job. But are we hearing Him?

According to acclaimed Bible teacher and author Ann Graham Lotz, daughter of evangelist Billy Graham, "Learning to recognize the voice of God is critical, not only for our own peace of mind but also for developing a personal relationship with Him." That's so true; we simply cannot develop intimacy with Him if we're doing all the talking. It would be like going on a date with a guy afflicted with diarrhea of the mouth and never getting one word in edgewise.

We must hear Papa God speak to us and hear Him clearly.

MAY I ASK WHO'S CALLING?

In the third chapter of 1 Samuel, a mere boy demonstrates how hearing and responding to that divine voice speaking to us is essential to growing our faith. Young Samuel had never before heard the voice of Yahweh, so at first he didn't recognize it. But through Samuel's knowledge of scripture and blossoming trust, with a little tutelage and encouragement from his mentor, he began learning to discern the voice of Papa God. His willingness to listen and obey launched a deep personal relationship that affected not only his life but also an entire nation.

Samuel came to know what he didn't know because of what he did know. And so do we.

Because our judgment in this compass-resistant, gray-shaded, create-your-own-values world is vulnerable to being skewed by the influence of Satan, the Great Deceiver, we have to constantly ask ourselves, "Whose voice are we listening to? Are we tuning into the Holy Spirit or. . .someone else?"

Think for a moment about the account of mankind's fall into sin in the book of Genesis. The paint was barely dry on creation when we marred it by bad decisions. We didn't even make it two whole chapters before we got voted off the island.

After Adam and Eve had allowed themselves to be swayed by Satan's clever lies and made the choice to sin by directly disobeying their Creator, they became overcome with shame about their newly discovered nakedness (which was as much spiritual nakedness as physical).

Cue the face-off: "When the cool evening breezes were blowing, the man and his wife heard the LORD God walking about in the garden. So they hid from the LORD God among the trees" (Genesis 3:8 NLT).

First of all, I think it's way beyond cool that Papa God would take on human form with walking appendages like ours (and I'll assume the rest of the body, too) to swing by for a visit. Yep, God grew legs for the occasion. I wonder if He looked like Jesus. Hey, can you imagine what you'd do if you were vacuuming in the buff one day and the all-powerful Master of heaven and earth showed up on your doorstep for a neighborly chat over chai tea and moon pies?

Adam and Eve did what you and I would probably have done. They fled. As we say in the South, they parked their nekked hinnies behind the chrysanthemums. (Okay, maybe I'm the only one who says that.) They were trying to hide more than their guilt.

"Who told you that you were naked?" Yahweh responded to Adam when he hollered from the bushes that he and the little missus weren't appropriately dressed for company (Genesis 3:11 NLT).

Don't you *hate* it when drop-ins catch you with rollers in your hair, torn sweats, and no makeup?

Papa already knew the answer to His question, of course, but He was trying to get the original first couple—and us—to consider the true source of our choices. Who exactly are we listening to? Is it Him? Our own selfish egos? Or maybe a hideous, hulking spiritual outcast squished into a scaly serpent suit?

We must discern and decide.

So how do we know if it truly is Yahweh speaking to us? Papa's guidance isn't bolded, italicized, or scripted in glittery gold calligraphy. His voice isn't loud, deep, or accompanied by tympani. In fact, it looks like any other written word and sounds an awful lot like any other thought. There's no flowery King James English with thees and thous and whithersoevers. The Almighty's voice is, in fact, still and small and ever so gentle. Even humble. I've heard Him referred to as the ultimate gentleman.

Many people mistake Papa's voice for conscience. But the difference is intent; heart motivation. Papa's focus is almost always on you helping others—representing Him as His loving hands and feet on earth. If the voice you hear is all about you, hang up; you've got a wrong number.

Another litmus test for voice filtering is that the Holy Spirit will never lead us contrary to scripture.

If a little inner voice is telling you it's okay to fudge on your income tax (everybody does it) or tell an untruth (it's just a harmless little white one) or take the hotel towel (after all, they have thousands), you can bet your stash of Cadbury that it's not the Holy Spirit talking. He will never condone cheating, lying, or stealing in any form. Never.

That's why studying the Bible to know precisely what is and isn't acceptable to God is essential in developing discernment. Then we can't be deceived because we know the truth.

SNEAKY AND SLIMY

If God's truth isn't imbedded in our hearts and minds, a shrewd and conniving enemy (Satan rarely dons his serpent costume these days; he has more success disguised as something enticingly beautiful) can influence our thinking and therefore our actions, even our dreams and goals. His interferences weigh heavily on whether we think specific personal goals—the goals Papa God has implanted within us—are possible for us to attain or not. I mean, why bother trying to fulfill a dream if seems unattainable?

So instead we do nothing. We end up stagnating like slimy green swamp scum when we could have been skimming along to exciting destinations on life's airboat.

This is really important, sister. Our lives may be drastically altered by listening to the wrong voice. Let us become too wise to buy lies.

Satan's attacks can be sneaky and clever. When Christian author Rebekah Montgomery was in the middle of launching her new book, *Faith Prints*, her e-mail account was hacked, and everyone on her church contact list received a note from Rebekah that said, "I think you're fat." Many, especially those who didn't know her well, didn't realize it was bogus and were very upset. The misunderstanding wreaked havoc.

Another sniveling, surreptitious scheme of the devil: if Satan can't make us sinful, he'll make us busy. It's wicked brilliant, really. There's no better way to distract us from keeping our eyes on Jesus; we're preoccupied with our to-do lists, deadlines, and being productive (my own personal nemesis). It never occurs to us to consult the Holy Spirit when decisions arise. We forget to pray, forsake daily face time with Papa, and neglect to feed our faith. And if we don't keep our faith well nourished, it'll eventually wither and die.

We mustn't get so busy that we forget the things that are truly important.

But hey, no need to fret about one thing at least—we now have iPhone apps to keep track of our sins.[10] Yep, it's come to that. The Ten Commandments are listed with a check box for your repentance convenience. Wonder what to do if you gluttonize an entire strawberry cheesecake—not that you or I would do such a thing, of course. At least not during the past ten minutes. "Thou shalt not pig out" isn't on the i-list. But sin is sin.

And considering the incriminating red evidence smeared on my face (didn't say what I was doing fifteen minutes ago), Proverbs 10:13 takes on new meaning: "Wisdom is found on the lips of the discerning" (NIV).

Discernment is immensely important in relationships, especially in marriage. These days, a rocky marriage is far more common than a marriage that rocks. Discerning intent is crucial when we're tempted to blast Spouse for something he did that we found hurtful. Perhaps the results of his action turned out badly, but what was his true intention?

CASE IN POINT: THE PHILODENDRON FIASCO

I truly love my man, Chuck. I do. But sometimes the way he thinks completely baffles me.

One day he got a hankering to do yard work. That in itself was phenomenal. So out he went to mow, trim, weed-whack, and leaf-blow. When he came in, sweaty and filthy from head to toe, he informed me with a gleam of pride in his eye that he'd tidied up the backyard flower bed for me and fixed the sprinkler problem.

Sprinkler problem? There was no sprinkler problem. Uh-oh. I began to get a bad inkling.

Now you first have to understand that although the lawn is Chuck's job, the flower beds are my domain. I plan, plant, and carefully nurture each and every flower, shrub, and ornamental. I often talk to them and sometimes even sing to them. Don't laugh. They're my little green babies.

So imagine my absolute horror when I walked out the back door to find my gorgeous six-foot split-leaf philodendron stretched out like a dead body beside the garbage can. It had been hacked off at the base.

I was so devastated I could barely breathe as I stood staring at the huge gaping hole in the row of enormous, wondrously healthy philodendrons I had planted and lovingly coaxed to adulthood during the past three years. The one in the middle was missing. The one by the sprinkler head.

Chuck, with his logical see-a-problem-so-fix-it left brain, had decided the plant had grown so big that it was blocking the sprinkler. What he failed to consider was that the whole point of the sprinkler was to grow the plant big.

I cried. I actually wept for my murdered green baby. And then I got mad.

The rage fuse lit somewhere in my innards and erupted into

an inferno. I was ready to storm inside and blast the clueless cold-blooded murderer. But something stopped me. It was the Holy Spirit reminding me of Proverbs 18:2 (NIV): "Fools find no pleasure in understanding but delight in airing their own opinions."

To tell you the truth, I was so livid, I didn't much care whether I was a fool or not at that moment. But I knew Papa God did. So I just stood there praying for a new herspective, sobbing as quietly as I could so the neighbors wouldn't call the men in white jackets to haul me away.

Out of the corner of my eye, I noticed Chuck covertly watching me from the porch. My mind flew back to the funeral I had recently attended of a woman I'd known since I was a child. During the heart-squeezing eulogy, her husband of fifty-eight years praised the way she'd held their marriage together through difficult times and said in a grief-choked voice, "She never looked down on me in all those years. She always looked up at me in respect. . .even when I didn't deserve it. "

Then their forty-something daughter admitted that during her entire lifetime, she'd never heard her mother say one bad word about her father.

Whoa. Those words hit me hard. I was so convicted about the poor judgment I'd shown in criticizing my husband—much of it in my own mind—that I vowed to listen harder for the voice of the Holy Spirit guiding and helping me navigate the choppy waters of marriage.

So standing awkwardly in my backyard, I asked for better discernment. "Lord, help me understand him, not criticize him. Deep inside I know he meant well and was only trying to help me. Glue my mouth shut, Lord; help me forgive him and really appreciate all he does around the house."

Later that afternoon, I got up enough courage to go back out to the flower bed to attempt some damage control. To my surprise, there in the gap next to the stark green stump, stood my listing, drooping philodendron. Chuck had dug a hole and tried to replant the poor, rootless thing. He'd even watered it.

I burst into tears again, but this time they were warm tears of gratitude mingled with salty tears of joy. Oh, I knew there was no hope for the philodendron, but the point was that by me not blowing up and instead following the Holy Spirit's loving lead, what could have been a marital Hiroshima. . .wasn't.

And because of the Helper's intervention, Chuck got it. Without feeling criticized or belittled, he got that he'd unwittingly broken my heart and was doing his best to redeem the situation. How can you not love a guy like that?

Marriage counselor Dr. Gary Campbell says, "Love is a choice you make every day. And in choosing love, you're following Christ's example. Nothing is more Christlike than loving your spouse."[11]

And that's the bottom line of discernment—becoming more Christlike by making good decisions. Sound decisions. Godly decisions.

So the next time you're trying to figure out who gets the seat belt—your Diet Coke or your toddler—remember that although it's prudent to remain open to all possibilities, don't be so open-minded that your faith falls out.

It's not hard to make decisions when you know what your values are.
~ROY DISNEY

FOLLOWING MY PERSONAL GPS (GOD-POWERED SATELLITE)

1. Can you think of one decision you've made that likely would've turned out differently if you'd consulted the Holy Spirit for guidance?

2. Whose voice do you tend to listen to most when making decisions?

3. Look back at the definition of discernment on page 126; what do you think will give us an *enlightened perspective* so we can honestly judge what is and isn't from God?

4. What (or who) is buckled in, riding shotgun beside you? In other words, what (or who) is your top priority?

5. Is there anything going on in your marriage right now that you haven't asked for—and actively listened for—the Holy Spirit's guidance?

CHAPTER 15

Breakdown in the Fast Lane
(Depression)

He. . .has lifted up the humble.
LUKE 1:52 NIV

My friend Hannah was in the pits. Reeling from an unwanted divorce, she felt used up and discarded. The future looked grim, but she yearned for her life to count for something. She wanted, more than anything, to help hurting people. So although she had a degree in English literature and was a decade older than the average medical school applicant, at thirty-something, Hannah decided to become a doctor.

Being able to quote Walt Whitman didn't help much with the med school entrance requirements, and it was a struggle to beef up her anemic science background; but with a boatload of grit and determination, Hannah succeeded. In fact, she succeeded so well, she scored in the top 7 percent on the national medical board exams.

As if tough academics weren't enough to contend with, Hannah found herself falling in love, planning a wedding, learning to take care of a new husband and three busy stepchildren, and giving birth to a beautiful baby girl of her own, all during medical school.

Indeed, life was hectic, but Hannah loved it. She was on top of the world.

Then one day, Hannah's mountaintop avalanched.

While moving a heavy patient, she suddenly experienced acute back pain. She kept going though, performing her hospital duties, thinking it would surely subside, but it didn't. Wearing the mandatory heavy protective lead X-ray vests to perform diagnostic procedures added pressure on her slim frame and increased the pain in her spine. She tried physical therapy and analgesics, but pain in her hip and down her leg became excruciating.

Bad news. A spinal disc had ruptured and impinged spinal nerves. Surgery was necessary.

After three months flat on her back, Hannah began rehabilitation. But something was very wrong. When she tried to walk, she was shocked at the intense pain that slammed her leg; horrendous, stabbing, scream-producing neurological pain. It was even worse than she'd experienced before surgery. Nothing helped, although doctors tried every conceivable pain-control option. They couldn't even come up with a definitive diagnosis. This shouldn't be happening.

Hannah's vital, fulfilling, busy life ground to a halt.

The next two years were a nightmare. Because of the unmanageable pain, Hannah had to stop working. The doctor was now a patient. She felt completely hopeless. Her dreams were smashed, and her identity was lost both professionally and personally. She was unable to walk or drive and required help caring for her basic needs, much less the needs of her family. Once athletic and active, Hannah was now weak and dependent on a reclining electric wheelchair that she had to constantly adjust to find a tolerable position.

She felt stripped of everything that made her uniquely Hannah. She no longer recognized herself. Who was she if not a mother. . .a doctor. . .a busy woman? In the throes of despair, she cried out to God. A longtime believer, Hannah knew in her head that her heavenly Father would never leave or forsake her (Hebrews 13:5 again!), but her heart agonized over her loss of the life she once knew and loved.

She sank into depression.

Through all this time, despite her disappointment and disillusionment, she kept communication lines open with Papa God. Friends started a weekly Bible study at Hannah's home. They studied a topic Hannah hadn't thought about much in her pre-pain days: humility. An it's-not-about-me existence. "Humility is not about letting someone pass you in line at the grocery store," one of Hannah's soul sisters said to her. "It's about identity—the identity God is asking you to assume."

So began Hannah's search for her new identity. During her still ongoing quest, Hannah has discovered some profound truths I believe can help all of us with our own battles with depression. I've combined them with suggestions from other depression survivors (including myself) for the remainder of this chapter.

BLESS MY MESS

Life, by its very nature, is messy. Living organisms are made up of a complex structure of interdependent elements that are constantly adapting, moving, processing. We humans are the Master Designer's ultimate living organism, so we must expect some amount of flux to be present as long as we are alive. Change is inevitable.

Things would, of course, be considerably easier if we were fence posts.

But since we're organic, vital, vigorous beings—made in Papa God's image, mind you—we cannot expect weeds in our life gardens to tidily line up in neat little easy-to-pluck rows. Those weeds, in the form of illness, fluctuating finances, unforeseen job changes, damaged relationships, heartbreak—and yes, depression—will likely happen to each of us at some point. And when they do, we'll feel uncomfortable, discombobulated, and whacked out of control.

Our life will, for sure, seem indelibly messy.

Know what? Messy happens to all of us, so we mustn't allow ourselves to fall into the victim mentality trap. We are not being picked out to be picked on. And we will not sit back in our misery and allow messy to bury us alive. We will *do* something about it. We can be whelmed without being overwhelmed.

None of us is in this alone. Not even you.

Although when you're depressed you sometimes feel like the only dill pickle in a barrel of cucumbers, recognize that you're in good company. Many high achievers have had to deal with depression, including astronaut Buzz Aldrin, composer Ludwig van Beethoven, TV personality Drew Carey, US presidents Calvin Coolidge and Abraham Lincoln, Princess Diana, author J. K. Rowling, and actors Jim Carrey, Ashley Judd, Brooke Shields, and Emma Thompson. Even world-altering movers and shakers like Charles Dickens and Winston Churchill[12] have documented struggles with depression.

So it's pretty evident that depression doesn't prevent you from being productive. . .or influential. . .or successful. You'll have to find another excuse.

I'm sorry if that sounds abrasive, but the hard truth is that 7 percent of the US population is diagnosed with depression.[13] That's roughly one in every fourteen people. If everyone struggling with depression folded up and tucked themselves away until they felt ready to function again, we'd be a hollow, unproductive, weak nation full of hollow, unproductive, weak people.

ASSESS THEN ADDRESS YOUR MESS

So how do you continue functioning when you're depressed? Even though you absolutely don't feel like it?

Well, this is the time you need a strong support system, sister. Seek godly counseling and understanding Christian girlfriends at your church or Bible study. They'll gradually become heart friends. . . soul sisters who will join hands with you as you assess then address your mess. Through your combined strength, you'll pull through it with your faith eventually emerging even stronger than before.

Trust me, girlfriend, even during times of depression when we aren't very lovable, Papa never loves us less through our mess. He wants only to bless. These are not empty words; I know this from my own experience.

In my book, *Mom NEEDS Chocolate*, I tell the story of my first bout of depression as a young, newly married woman overcome by health and financial woes. (Believe it or not, Papa used a hilarious encounter with a jealous African lion as the catalyst to begin my healing process—you're gonna roar over this story if you've never heard it; starts on page 51 of *MNC*.)

I also share my two-year struggle with depression after my sixth heart-wrenching miscarriage in the "Lost and Found" chapter of *Too Blessed to Be Stressed* and how I found my way back to the faith I thought I'd lost. David's cries of despair became my prayers—the only ones I could muster—as I prayed through the Psalms (specific passages are listed in the book; so sorry, but I don't have space to repeat them all here).

Yahweh's Word seeped into my parched spirit like a cool spring of water and gradually, gently, healing and restoration came. "Do you want more and more of God's kindness and peace? Then learn to know him better and better" (2 Peter 1:2 TLB).

Another thing to consider is that depression is a manageable medical condition. Did you catch that noteworthy word, *medical?* The first step in dealing with depression is to see a physician to rule out a host of possible underlying causes or contributors, such as thyroid problems, hormonal imbalances, vitamin or mineral deficiencies (vitamins B12 and D have known ties to depression), or undiagnosed illnesses (stroke, cancer, diabetes, or Parkinson's disease to name a few). Then you decide together on a course of treatment and begin to manage your condition.

Medication and therapy with a trained Christian counselor help lots of women. Because of the fuzzy thinking and inability to make decisions many experience during depression, creating daily structure can also be cathartic; replacing aimlessness and lethargy with a simple schedule provides direction when we feel lost, focus when we're scattered, and the opportunity for accomplishment, be it ever so humble. (A whopper woohoo for checklists we can scratch off and then rip to shreds when everything is accomplished. I'm the reigning checklist queen!)

Eating a healthy, mood-boosting diet (that doesn't usually include caramel swirl brownies, although I've been known to occasionally indulge in this breakfast of champions), plus getting regular exercise and sunlight are all important weapons in combating depression.

And there are lots more "weapons" that space prohibits me from going into here. But if you're fighting depression, I encourage you to explore the wealth of good information available and pursue a course of action. Don't be a passive petunia, sister; be proactive!

MUZZLE THE SNARLING BEAST

If you recall, I mentioned Winston Churchill earlier in the list of famous people battling depression. Did you know that Mr. Churchill (somehow I just can't call him Winston; feels as weird as referring to Richard Nixon as Dick) called depression his "black dog"? He considered it a dark, razor-toothed, carnivorous force that hounded him, nipping at his heels most of his adult life.

I think that's absolutely brilliant, really.

Name it to tame it.

Giving depression an identity, a face, a physical form, makes it much easier to confront. By naming it, Mr. Churchill affirmed that his depression was an entity separate from himself and therefore could not define who he was. He was then able to view depression as an attacking creature to be subdued and tethered, not as a hopeless black hole that had swallowed his soul.

And hopelessness is depression's goal. Once you've begun to feel hopeless, the black dog is winning. It has you on the ground with its snarling, vicious, drooling mouth straddling your throat.

No! The battle isn't over. In your weakness, tap into Papa's immense strength and thrust your fingers into the black dog's molten eyes. Knee him in the knubees. Get off the ground. Slap that howling soul-sucker in a muzzle and cage him in the back forty.

In grateful humility, begin your quest for a new, messy-but-manageable identity.

But most of all, embrace hope for a better tomorrow. Stay tuned for more about hope in chapter 24, but for now, listen to one of my all-time favorite authors, Victor Hugo (who wrote *Les Misérables*): "Hope is the word which God has written on the brow of every man."

Having felt the black dog's penetrating fangs against my throat more than once, I absolutely believe in the transforming power of hope.

Hannah believes it from her wheelchair.

You, dear friend, can choose to believe it, too.

Hope is the feeling we have that the feeling we have is not permanent.
~MIGNON MCLAUGHLIN

FOLLOWING MY PERSONAL GPS (GOD-POWERED SATELLITE)

1. With what can you most identify in Hannah's struggle with depression? Just so you know, Hannah has found her new identity as a Bible teacher/mom/friend and is an active, vibrant, inspirational force in the lives of many (including me!). She still can't drive, walk, or dance in a sunbeam, but she zips around in her very cool electric wheelchair and despite nagging pain, enjoys her crazy, messy life. Now don't forget to answer the question!

2. What messy element of your life has nudged you toward depression? What did you do about it? How did you find your new normal—your new identity?

3. Does it help you to get a mental image of depression to better fight it off? If Mr. Churchill's black dog doesn't exactly fit your portrait of depression, what image do you envision?

4. What do you think of Victor Hugo's take on hope? When I first heard it I pictured a forehead tat, but I think he means something deeper than that. What are your thoughts about the role of hope in depression?

5. How will you handle that gal you come across today—the one you sense is secretly depressed? What can you suggest to help her?

CHAPTER 16

Dents in My Fender
(Collisions with Difficult People)

---

*If it is possible, as far as it depends on you,
live at peace with everyone.*
ROMANS 12:18 NIV

"You've gotta be kidding me, Lord," I muttered, recalling the scriptural mandate above. "Peace with everyone? *Everyone?* Even her?" I shook my head while eyeing the woman who'd just insulted me in front of thirty amused teens. Angry retorts on the tip of my tongue heated up like a blowtorch. I wanted to scorch her eyebrows off.

Okay, let me back up.

A local middle school administrator, who was a longtime friend and fan of my books, had asked me to speak during the first two periods of Mrs. Persimmon's (not her real name, of course) seventh-grade English class for the Great American Teach-In. I'd had to scuttle my schedule, but yes, I agreed to do it, remembering the dozens of rewarding times I'd spoken to students about writing in years past. And hey, what wouldn't I do for a fan?

So the Teach-In day arrived and I, along with numerous other tote-lugging adults of varying professions, trudged what seemed like five miles across the expansive campus to the school's media center to check in. There, we were each assigned a classroom and a reluctant student escort.

My escort was a gangly, curly-haired young man of thirteen who couldn't seem to find it within himself to make eye contact or answer any of my questions with more than one syllable. I couldn't hold it against him. I was young and shy once (oh yes I was!) and felt terribly awkward speaking to strange adults. And as grown-ups go, I guess I'm about as strange as they get.

He led and I followed, lugging several bulging cases containing my laptop, projector, books, and props. We finally made it around the bend, up the stairs, and down the never-ending hallway to my assigned classroom, only to find it dark and deserted. Hmm. Only fifteen minutes before my scheduled starting time, and I had specified to the administrator that I would need a minimum of fifteen minutes to set up.

"No problem," she had said. Well, it was a problem now.

"What should I do?" I asked my young escort.

He shrugged and tried the doorknob. Surprisingly, it turned. So he opened the door and we went in. Then without a word, he flipped on the light, turned, and left.

I waited an additional five minutes, but still no Mrs. Persimmon. As uncomfortable as I was, making myself at home in the classroom of someone I didn't know, I really didn't see any way around it. So I unpacked as students began trickling in.

And then the unthinkable happened. As I bent over to plug in my projector, the cord somehow got wrapped around a metallic piece of equipment about the size of my kitchen mixer that was sitting on the table and sent it crashing to the floor.

"Oooh, are you ever gonna get in trouuu-ble. . ." I heard from a cluster of bug-eyed boys who immediately gathered around the busted high-tech electronic device.

"Those things cost about a million dollars, I think."

"Mrs. Persimmon is sooo gonna blow."

"You better tell her you did it, lady, 'cause if she thinks it was one of us, we're dead meat."

I had no idea what I'd broken, but I had a sinking feeling that it was an iceberg and I was the *Titanic.*

At that moment, the bell rang and Mrs. Persimmon finally made her entrance. She marched directly over to me with lips pursed, glanced up at the PowerPoint slide I was attempting to center on the wall screen, and snapped, "Who are you? What is this? Who let you in here?"

Taken aback, I replied, "I'm Debora Coty, an author. I'm sorry . . .didn't the administrator tell you I'd be speaking to your class today? The door was unlocked but no one was here to meet me so I started getting my presentation ready."

"I don't know anything about it," she said curtly. With that, she spun on her heels and marched over to her desk across the room, where she turned her back and began typing on her computer. (I learned later that the administrator had previously sent her two e-mails and a voice mail about me coming.)

Thirty students sat mutely staring at me, and I back at them. What was I supposed to do now?

My attention was drawn to the pathetic, broken high-tech mixer-thingie sitting on the table. A jagged-edged boulder began forming somewhere in my gut. I knew before anything else happened, I had to do the right thing, if nothing more than to be an example to thirty impressionable kids who were waiting to see how this would play out.

So I inched over to her desk, feeling very much like a delinquent seventh grader. "Mrs. Persimmon," I said in a voice that sounded strangely wobbly, "I need to tell you something. While I was setting up, that piece of equipment over there got knocked off onto the floor and appears to be broken. It was an accident, and I'm truly very sorry. I'll be glad to pay for—"

"WHAT?" she shouted. "You BROKE it?" Mrs. Persimmon's eyes grew to the size of Frisbees as she took in the electronic gizmo with its little head cocked askew. Her face turned three shades of maroon as she leaped to her feet.

"Do you have any idea how much they cost? I don't know if we have any more, and I use it every day. I can't BELIEVE you broke it. HOW could you be so clumsy? This is TERRIBLE! Just TERRIBLE!"

On and on she went, alternating between fussing, yelling, and berating me. Right there in front of the students. As if I were a bad dog who'd lifted my leg on her carpet. She just couldn't get past it and move on. . .the more she stormed, the madder she got.

Then suddenly, like a heavy brocade curtain dropping on Act I, she halted in mid-rant, turned to the class, and said in a barely controlled voice, "Today is the Great American Teach-In. This lady is apparently here to talk to you about whatever it is she does." She pivoted and returned to her desk. We all gawked at the back of her head as she began pounding an agitated rhythm on her computer keys.

So the ball was in my court. I felt about two inches tall. I was a bad girl. *Bad, bad* girl. And everyone there knew it.

My first impulse was to escape. To pack up my things, take my toys, and go home. I didn't need this. I'd made a mistake, yes, a very bad one I expected to pay dearly for, but I didn't deserve to be humiliated. I was twenty years older than Mrs. Persimmon; shouldn't that garner a little respect? But thirty pairs of adolescent eyes were looking expectantly at me. I couldn't tell if they were waiting to see me burst into tears (which I feared might happen at any moment) or if they truly wanted to see how a grown-up should handle an embarrassing situation.

When did I become so grown-up anyway? Wrinkles and cellulite do not maturity make. I may be fifty-something on the outside, but on the inside I'm often still a kid. This, however, was a time I knew I had to act like a mature child of the almighty King, whether I felt like it or not.

So with face blazing, I fumbled forward. The presentation was the most flustered, disjointed one I've ever given, but at least I made it through to the end. And oddly enough, the kids seemed to love it.

SAME SONG, DIFFERENT VERSE

Mrs. Persimmon, who had kept typing nonstop with her back to me during my entire program, remained frosty when the bell rang and the first set of students was exchanged for another. She ignored me as the incoming students took their seats. Why, oh why, had I agreed to speak to two classes?

"Get out your books and read," the new class was instructed as I stood in front waiting to be introduced and begin my next presentation. After five minutes, I finally sat down. My PowerPoint was fifty minutes long, so I needed to start ASAP if I was going to have a prayer of finishing, but on they read. No explanation or instruction was forthcoming from Mrs. Persimmon. She continued to peck at her keyboard as if I didn't exist.

When ten minutes had ticked away, I approached her desk and asked how much longer it would be until I could begin.

Sheepishly, she answered, "A few more minutes. I guess I should have told you that this group always reads during the first portion of class."

"That would have been good to know, yes," I replied, stony-faced.

Looking directly into my eyes for the first time since our explosive encounter, she added in an almost-pleasant tone, "By the way, the media specialist just e-mailed that the broken equipment can be replaced immediately, so everything will turn out fine."

"Well, I'm very glad to hear it," I said, resisting the temptation to say, "Fine? You call the humiliation you've caused me *fine*?" Try as I might, I was having a horrendous time not biting back with the same hostile tone with which she'd earlier lambasted me. I wanted so badly to tell her just how rude she'd been and that I would never, ever, *ever* do another classroom presentation because of her.

But in a flash of insight, I knew that words spoken in anger would make the best retort I would ever regret. If I reacted rather than responded, I'd actually become the sniveling, all-about-me adolescent I felt like at that moment. I had to let this anger go. I needed to BARF.

WHEN YOU'RE ANGRY ENOUGH TO BARF, DO IT

BARF is the anger management tool I introduced in my book, *More Beauty, Less Beast* (see the "Melted Earrings" chapter for details on this and other defusing techniques). It's an acronym that stands for:

B: Back Off
A: Admit
R: Redirect
F: Forgive

So I BARFed. As the students continued reading, I excused myself to the restroom (backed off by putting physical distance between my offender and myself), where I promptly admitted to a roll of toilet paper that I felt so disrespected and belittled that I wanted to stuff its very self where the sun doesn't shine on Persimmons.

After closing my eyes and taking three deep breaths, I redirected my thoughts to my Life Saver verse of the month, which was, by Papa's sly divine appointment, Proverbs 25:15 (NIV): "A gentle tongue can break a bone." The irony made me laugh. I felt the jagged boulder in my gut crack in two.

Then with my blood pressure nearly normalized, I returned to the classroom and finished my presentation.

NUTS, DENTS, AND HOLES

I'd like to say forgiving Mrs. Persimmon was a cakewalk, but to be honest, it took another two weeks before I could think of her without my derriere cheeks clinching.

Graciousness is the hardest thing in the world to come by in responding to ungracious people, isn't it? I call them nuts in my batter. Dents in my fender. Holes in my Nikes.

But consider that word, gracious. Our commonly perceived definition is "exhibiting kindness and courtesy." Any ol' body can do that. Why, we Southern gals are raised to behave courteously even if we're mad as a riled hornet (which is most of the time). This type of graciousness is strictly external, like peach fuzz. We don't feel gracious, but we pretend because it's the polite thing to do.

I can't help but wonder amid all this deceit if there's a spiritual element to authentic biblical graciousness. Some sort of sweetness generated by Papa God to infuse the pulp of peachy me that has nothing to do with faux external fuzz courtesy. In other words, is there motivation to be gracious that goes deeper than simply behaving respectably?

Sure enough, there is.

Webster adds "godly" and "compassionate" and "generosity of spirit" to the portrait of true graciousness. These spiritual attributes bring us to the root of graciousness, which is, of course, grace. As in Papa God's grace toward us in that while we were yet sinners He sent Christ, His one and only Son—the only perfect, sinless Person who ever lived—to die in our place (Romans 5:8).

As in His amazing grace that sets us free from the fear of condemnation because we, too, like our offenders, mess up sometimes (Romans 6:15).

Once we can understand and embrace the magnitude and breadth of His divine grace, our peachy inner pulp becomes sweeter and sweeter, reflecting the nature of Papa within us. It's because of His grace toward us that we can extend grace to others.

Forget the faux fuzz.

GRACE IN YOUR FACE

I absolutely love the definition of grace in The Message translation of Romans 5:20: "Aggressive forgiveness." Say that phrase aloud with me: aggressive forgiveness. Now slowly, considering the meaning of each word: Aggressive. Forgiveness. At first blush, it sounds like an oxymoron, but isn't that a marvelous way to look at grace? It's not some wimpy, limp, passive behavior in which we pretend to be kind and overlook wrongs done to us when they're really just festering beneath the fuzz.

Grace is strong, aggressive, determined pursuit. It's not allowing resentment to fester any longer but facing those wrongs and actively pursuing forgiveness.

Those traits are exactly what we need to extend grace to

those who step on or take advantage of us. . .we must be strong, aggressive—the step beyond assertive—and determined. It means not to retaliate but to get past our stubborn pride and forgive.

Did you know we get an awesome return on our investment once we do? In Proverbs 25:21–22, we're assured that if we extend grace and treat our enemy with kindness, "You will heap coals of fire on his head, and the LORD will reward you" (NKJV). Too cool. I'd think the burning charcoal nest on our offender's noggin would be reward enough for us, but there's an *and* there. . . . : "*and* the Lord will reward you." Prodigious! I'll never turn down an additional grace note in my life, will you?

Oh, let me add another important thing here: you don't have to become BFFs with your offender after you've forgiven him or her. With some people, you must simply extend Papa's grace and then move on. If you were close previously, the relationship may not be fully restored. Don't wallow in guilt. You've done your job. You may have to forge a different relationship with that person based on grace, and that's okay. We weren't meant to be besties with everyone.

There may be occasions when our offender refuses to accept the grace we offer. In that case, we should follow Jesus' mandate to His disciples when He sent them out to extend grace through the gospel: "Whoever will not receive you nor hear your words, when you depart from that house or city, shake off the dust from your feet" (Matthew 10:14 NKJV).

In modern vernacular, hit the road, Jack. *Hasta la vista*, baby. Don't let the door hit you in the bum. Once you've sincerely offered the olive branch but they refuse to accept it, they are no longer your responsibility. Their offense is now between them and Papa God. He will dole out those hot coals in His own time and way.

So blowtorching eyebrows really isn't a good idea. Papa has

a much better plan: grace. After all, we mustn't deprive the Persimmons of this world their hot coal–induced hairdo bonfire. I'll bring the marshmallows and Hershey's if you bring the grahams.

People who fly into a rage always make a bad landing.
~WILL ROGERS

FOLLOWING MY PERSONAL GPS (GOD-POWERED SATELLITE)

1. I've heard it said, "You don't have to attend every argument you're invited to," but some of us find many such invitations difficult to turn down. How about you—can you usually walk away from a fight in the making?

2. Even Paul and Barnabas got into a "sharp disagreement" and went their separate ways (Acts 15:39 NIV). When do you think it's justifiable to agree to disagree and part company?

3. Even if you're not a Southerner, are you adept at peach fuzz forgiveness (external only—just to be polite)? When did you last perform peach fuzz forgiveness?

4. Romans 6:15 promises us, "God's grace has set us free" (NLT). How can you dig deeper into the peachy pulp to tap into the freedom generated by genuine biblical graciousness and forgiveness?

5. Has anyone refused to accept the grace you've offered? How did you deal with it?

CHAPTER 17

Reinflating Flat Tires
(Personal Restoration)

———————※———————

God is our refuge and strength,
always ready to help in times of trouble.
PSALM 46:1 NLT

||||||||||||||||||||||||||||||||||||||||||||||||||||||||||||||||||||||||||||||||||||||||||||||||||||||||||||||||||||||||||||||

If you've read any of my other books, you already know about my relationship with my four-wheeler, Sir Lancelot. Lance, who resides at our remote Smoky Mountain cabin, is my mountaintop prayer partner. Some of my very best face time with the Almighty has been atop good ol' Lance as I relish Papa God's beautiful mountaintop cathedral, listening for His still, small voice, basking in His presence, and thanking Him for the magnificence of His creation.

But sometimes my twenty-first-century steed can't pull his weight. Or mine. It's because of a flat tire. He tries to hobble along on his lame leg, but nothing works right. He lurches so severely that he either throws me off the saddle or careens dangerously near the edge of a cliff. Neither makes for a jolly good time, believe you me.

It's the oddest thing, really; it's always the same tire but it's not all the time. Some mornings, for no apparent reason, he wakes up flat as a flitter (this is an expression I've heard all my life but I'm not really sure what a flitter is; I picture it somewhere between a pancake and crepe).

The point is: Lance simply cannot function as he was intended until he's been reinflated.

We women are much the same way. We, too, wake up some mornings with a flat tire. Or should I say with a spirit that's flat-out tired? We can try to limp along for days, even weeks or sometimes months, but when we're deflated, nothing works right. Everything's out of kilter on our insides and often our outsides as well.

In order to function the way we were intended—living a joyful, abundant, fulfilled life—we must pause upon occasion to be reinflated. Pumped up. Refreshed.

I call these crucial periods of rejuvenation He and Me Retreats. I first introduced the idea in *More Beauty, Less Beast*. He and Me Retreats can last three hours or three days, but they're basically an intentional, extended time away from the stress of your hustling, bustling life for face time with your loving Papa God.

It's so much easier to hear His still, small voice when you hit the mute button on life.

Jesus often stole away alone for prayer and renewal. His favorite retreat sites were immersed in nature, often the lake or the sea (Matthew 13:1) and the mountains (Mark 6:46). As you can tell by my Lance story, my fave is also the mountains. And my friends Carol and Julie feel the same way. Oh, you're just going to love their story.

THE HARDEST PART OF A JOURNEY
IS THE FIRST STEP

Carol had been feeling more and more deflated since her fiftieth birthday. Besides the constant stress of caring for a mentally ill son, chronic hip and shoulder pain from rheumatoid arthritis was really getting her down. The medicine prescribed by her rheumatologist produced awful side effects, so she stopped taking it. Some days she could barely move. The discomfort seemed unbearable.

Carol felt a deep longing for a spiritual journey, to step away from her problems and experience healing in her weary heart and aching body. But she didn't know how.

Then one day Carol's mother told her about an amazing spiritual pilgrimage she'd learned about at her church—a trail used for centuries as a soul-searching retreat for people seeking a closer walk with God. It sounded like the perfect answer to Carol's prayer. But there were a few major hitches: the Camino de Santiago (which means "The Way of Saint James") was in Spain and involved hiking hundreds of miles across mountainous terrain.

How could Carol, whose joints were acutely painful, possibly make such a journey? It was out of the question. Crazy. No way. Delete idea.

But for some reason, Carol just couldn't let it go. Every time she prayed for help and restoration, the Camino de Santiago popped into her head. Could Papa God really want her to try such a foolhardy thing?

Carol's decision was made when her mom, Julie, a seventy-four-year-old widow, offered to go with her. They would make the trek together, mother and daughter. Carol was deeply moved. "My mother taught me to walk, and I have been walking with her for fifty years." How could she not seize the opportunity for what might well be their final great adventure on earth together?

So training began. Julie drove five hundred miles so she and Carol could walk together every day for two months. They did short distances at first, which was excruciating for Carol because of her debilitating arthritis pain. Little by little, encouraging each other, they were able to increase their distance until they were walking six to eight miles daily.

When Julie returned to her home in Georgia, the two had finished purchasing all the gear for their trip, which they would each need to somehow consolidate onto one backpack. *One backpack!* Oh. My. Heavens. Can you even begin to fathom how to do that?

As a challenged packer, compiling and wearing three weeks' worth of luggage on my back would be my worst nightmare. But I'm an eyewitness that they did it. Their bulging backpacks strained like size 8 jeans over a size 12 tushie, but by dingies, they did it.

Training continued, but separately now. They hiked miles and miles through rain, heat, or humidity wearing their eighteen-pound backpacks. Carol's painful arthritic shoulders gradually adjusted to the weight of the load, and her hips didn't scream quite as loudly after a few weeks. Julie (remember she's seventy-four!) even walked eight miles, wearing her pack, to the local YMCA to participate in an exercise class, then back home again.

Both went through several pairs of shoes before finding a pair that didn't blister. They tried out all the gear and treated their backpacks, stuff sacks, bedding, and jackets to prevent bedbugs (a real risk on the Camino). Researching the trip took time, and they phoned each other daily to discuss every little detail of their travel plans. They had to get this right the first time. There would be no one to meet them, guide them, or help them in Spain. They would be completely on their own.

IS THIS REALLY HAPPENING?

Departure day arrived, and both Carol and Julie were nervous. Was this really a good idea? Although Carol's husband supported the venture in every way, neither of our girls felt ready. So as they had throughout eight months of grueling preparation, they prayed. Should they go through with it? Was it really the Lord's will for them to travel halfway around the world where they didn't speak the language and knew no one at all, for the sole purpose of hiking the equivalent of the state of Connecticut?

If you know Papa God like I know Papa God, you already

know the answer. He loves to show us there's no such thing as impossible when He's on our team.

They boarded the plane.

After a complicated schedule of plane, bus, shuttle, and train rides, they found themselves, along with other pilgrims from all over the world, following little yellow signs pointing directions along the portion of the Camino from the Spanish city of Leon to their final destination, Santiago de Compostela.

It was a humbling experience, being greeted by other travelers with, "Buen Camino," while treading the very path traveled over the centuries by kings and queens, Charlemagne, St. Francis of Assisi, and many, many others driven to seek the peace and joy that comes from a deeper relationship with their Savior. People willing to work and sacrifice to attain it.

Each morning, after rising from their beds in hostels or hotels on the Camino, they started the day with the prayer Carol wrote:

Morning Prayer
Good morning, God.
We love You and thank You for this new day.
Walk with us, and be our strength.
Let the Holy Spirit remind us throughout the day
of the beauty You have created on this earth and all around us;
in the people we meet and in all of our circumstances.
Let others see You in us today, and
may we see You in others;
may we all find peace in Your love.
Amen.

Many uphill, rocky sections of the Camino were immensely challenging, and our girls were so exhausted all they could do was look at each other and agree, "This is hard." They just kept putting one foot in front of the other. They stumbled. They faltered. They depended on each other as never before. Ecclesiastes 4:10 sprang to life: "If you fall, your friend can help you up. But if you fall without having a friend nearby, you are really in trouble" (CEV).

During the hardest climbs, Carol admits, "We would stop and turn around and feel amazed at how far we had come and be in awe of the incredible view from our new height. That helped us to turn back around and take another step toward our goal."

THE PINNACLE

When they reached the highest point on the Camino, Carol paused at La Cruz de Ferro, a huge iron cross erected on a mountainous overlook. There she prayed for her troubled son as she placed a stone she'd brought from home atop a pile, where for centuries people have carried stones symbolizing their burdens and left them at the foot of the cross. Nowadays, pilgrims also leave personal items, photos, letters, and written prayers for their loved ones.

It was a profound spiritual moment for Carol as she gave her burden to the Lord.

During the eighteen days they covered two hundred miles on the Camino, Carol wrote in her journal every day, beginning by listing three things for which she was thankful. By recognizing her blessings, although the way was difficult and her arthritic joints often throbbed, she found that God gave her the strength she needed to endure again and again. "He showed me that I could handle this. And that I'm stronger than I knew. My arthritis pain diminished when I began walking regularly. I never realized how much walking could help me."

Carol did receive the renewal she'd gone searching for, both spiritually and physically. Oh, she still has RA issues at times, but she is much more functional than before. And the memories and lessons she learned from her He and Me Retreat will remain with her always, summarized in the tender words of a prayer she and Julie found at a small church atop a mountain in O'Cebrerio written in several languages. Here is an excerpt we can all take to heart:

Although I may have shared all my possessions with people of other languages and cultures. . .if I am not capable of forgiving my neighbor tomorrow, I have arrived nowhere.
Although I may have seen all the mountains and contemplated the best sunsets. . .if I have not discovered who is the author of so much free beauty and so much peace, I have arrived nowhere.
If from today I do not continue walking on Your path, searching and learning according to what I have learned; if from today I have not seen in every person, friend or foe, a companion on the Camino; if from today I cannot recognize God, the God of Jesus of Nazareth, as the one God of my life, I have arrived nowhere.
~ FRAY DINO

How about you, sister—are you ready to leave your flitter-flatness behind and seek your own Camino? To actively pursue rejuvenation with the peace and joy that comes from a closer walk with Papa God? Your Camino doesn't have to be in Spain. You don't have to hike. It doesn't even have to be with your mother (okay, I heard that sigh of relief!). It's between you and Papa where it is. . .as long as it *is*.

Don't put it off.

Faith is putting all your eggs in God's basket, then counting your blessings before they hatch.
~RAMONA C. CARROLL

FOLLOWING MY PERSONAL GPS (GOD-POWERED SATELLITE)

1. On a scale of one (no air) to ten (fully inflated), how flat is your flitter gauge? Do your spiritual tires need pumping up a bit? Remember you, like Lance, can't function as you were intended when you're deflated. Stop right now and seriously consider a He and Me Retreat for yourself. . . Where could you go? When? What's stopping you? Listen, girlfriend, even debilitating arthritic pain didn't stop Carol; are you going to let a few obstacles stop you?

2. Hop back to page 157 and read Carol's morning prayer aloud. Now if that doesn't light your fire, your wood's wet. What would you think about creating your own personal morning prayer (or you can borrow Carol's) so you, too, can start each day chatting with your Papa?

3. While climbing the steepest cliffs of the Camino, Carol said, "We would stop and turn around and feel amazed at how far we had come and be in awe of the incredible view from our new height. That helped us to turn back around and take another step toward our goal." How can you apply this wise strategy to tackling the hardest climbs in your own life? What mountains are you currently facing right now?

4. Carol placed a stone symbolizing her burden for her son at the foot of the iron cross on the mountain. She didn't set it down and then pick it back up and continue carrying it as we women tend to do. She left it there. Do you have any stones weighing your spirit down that you need to leave at the foot of the cross today?

5. What portion of the O'Cebrerio church prayer speaks to you most? What's your destination for your current spiritual journey? Do you feel like you're moving closer to actually arriving. . .or are you going nowhere? What can you do to make sure that you keep moving forward?

CHAPTER 18

No More Horn-Cussing
(Forgiveness)

---

*With the LORD is unfailing love
and with him is full redemption.*
PSALM 130:7 NIV

||||||||||||||||||||||||||||||||||||||||||||||||||||||||||||||||||||||||||||||||||||||||||||||||||||||||||||||||||||||||||||||||

One Sunday morning not long ago, I was bedecked in my over-sized flowered hat adorned with a "Bible Story Lady" sign, leading a dozen two-and-a-half-year-olds in a rousing chorus of the "Prayer Song" before launching into our Bible story. Our lesson that day was, "When someone is mean to you, you don't have to be mean back."

Not exactly the deep end of the theology pool, I'll admit, but hey, everyone in my audience is shorter than my belly button. That's why I accepted this job in the first place—no PhD required. Just KISS and tell (KISS = Keep It Simple, Sister!).

There's this one kid in the class—a big boy for his age—who never sits in his chair. Well, he starts out there, but within minutes he's up and migrating with the wind currents around the room. Let's call him Danny (because if I use his real name, I'm toast).

So that morning I was deep into the hand motions of the song with everyone in the room singing along (except Danny), when my laid-back, sweet, adorable grandson Blaine arrived. No surprise there; his momma made us late for church every Sunday for eighteen years. There wasn't a single chair open in the room except the one Danny vacated. So the teacher directed Blaine to the empty chair, told him to sit, and walked away.

Blaine Boy had no sooner situated his adorable little self in the miniature red chair and flashed his hundred-watt smile at Mimi (me!)—still up front leading the song—than Danny's migration pattern came to a screeching halt. He'd noticed someone sitting in his chair. Not that he wanted to sit in it, mind you; he just didn't want anyone else to.

So with a running start from across the room, Danny charged sweet, unsuspecting, adorable Blaine and walloped him with a flying full-body slam, knocking him off the chair and sending him crashing onto the floor.

I witnessed the whole thing in slow-mo and could do absolutely nothing without stopping the song and disrupting the entire class. I helplessly watched the kid I cherish ever so much more than a crateful of Godiva get pummeled by a bully in training pants.

The spike in my blood pressure zapped my hair into a blond fro. I could feel my fillings begin to bubble. It was all I could do not to fly out of my seat and throttle that horrible little dweeb. I reminded myself that I'm the grown-up here, and he's only two. But hey, he looks three.

It didn't help. There's no shelf life on indignity. I was livid.

Little Blaine, looking dazed and confused, slowly rose to his feet and stood there eyeing Danny, obviously not understanding what had happened or what to do next. Danny glared back at him and climbed into the chair.

Squatter's rights. Survival of the nastiest. You lose, sucker.

Blaine's adorable little face began to pucker, and his bottom lip trembled. My guts were burning with the molten lava of injustice.

The volcano was about to blow. I was gonna clean little Danny's clock.

And then it hit me. An instant message coming straight from Papa God.

"Helloooo. When someone is mean to you (or in this case, your adorable little grandson), you don't have to be mean back."

But I *want* to be mean back, Lord. Danny deserves it.

"Doesn't matter. When someone is mean to you, you don't have to be mean back. I wasn't mean back when they beat Me up and shredded My skin with whips and thrust a crown of thorns on My head. Aren't you supposed to be becoming more like Me?"

Oh. Yeah. I guess.

At that point, the teacher brought a chair in from another room and helped Blaine into it. His little body shuddered as he fought big fat alligator tears threatening to squeeze between his eyelids. He was successful. He was brave. He was adorable. He gave Mimi a shaky smile and began to join in the hand motions of the song that Mimi felt would never, ever end.

Danny was off the chair again, paying no attention to the song. Then came that familiar still, small voice speaking once again to my heart.

"So Deb, now it's time to forgive Danny."

Maybe later, Lord. After I bring him up front and announce, "Okay class, here's a prime example of our lesson today. This is a bully. A mean, bad, rotten little boy. He shoved Blaine off the chair, but Blaine chose not to be mean back. Who does Papa God love more?"

"I love Danny as much as I love Blaine."

Yeah, well, he can't get away with busting up my grandbuddy. Someone needs to punish this kid. Maybe if I humiliate him in front of the class he'll learn his lesson.

"You know you can't do that. He made a mistake. Don't you ever make mistakes?"

I think I'm about to right now.

"But you won't. Because you love Me. And I love you. And we both love children who are learning to love Me, too. Now forgive Danny."

I can't, Lord. It's just too hard to forgive when someone you love has been hurt.

"Of course it's hard. That's why I'm here. I'll help you. Let's do this thing. And I'll give you an A+ on today's lesson. Let's say it together: When someone is mean to you, you don't have to be mean back."

[Heavy sigh] Got it.

"Good."

FORGIVENESS STARTS IN THE HEAD BUT ENDS IN THE HEART

Okay, so I'm lousy at this thing called forgiveness, but thankfully, it's a skill that improves with practice. Sometimes it's hard to remember that how we feel has nothing to do with forgiveness. Forgiveness starts in the head but ends in the heart. We forgive as an act of the will, because Papa God commands us to, not because of our feelings. If we wait until we feel like forgiving, we'll never forgive anybody. We'll just go on being consumed by resentment for the rest of our lives.

The actual act of forgiveness comes first; compassion and mercy are often secondary. Put another way, we must demonstrate forgiveness to feel forgiveness.

Forgiveness is like losing weight. It takes a combination of work, willfulness, and willpower to pull it off. A supreme effort, really. But once you succeed, you're the one who benefits most. You, not your offender. The person you forgive is released from the time-out chair, sure, but you're sprung from a cell on death row. "When you are praying, first forgive anyone you are holding a grudge against, so that your Father in heaven will forgive your sins, too" (Mark 11:25 NLT).

Forgiveness isn't really optional for believers; for us to receive forgiveness, we must give it. It's the only way to clear the communication lines of static and keep our fellowship with Papa God free of tower blockages and dropped calls. (In case you were wondering, the definition of fellowship is two fellows on one ship— pretty miserable if you don't get along.)

WOUNDED BY FRIENDLY FIRE

But you and I both know how difficult forgiveness can be when we've been cut to the bone and our wound just won't stop bleeding. It happens within families all the time, and it's the hardest thing in the world to forgive an offender who is thrust upon you at every holiday, wedding, or family gathering.

Someone who's supposed to be on your team. . .your own flesh and blood. . .your "loved one."

Forgiveness in the wake of friendly fire (the military term for a soldier shot by someone in her own army) is probably even harder than forgiving someone we don't know because we feel the injustice repeatedly, new and fresh, every time we're subjected to the chafing presence of the unrepentant offender. We want to grind Cousin Henry's abusive tongue into his pumpkin pie and submerge his sneering face in giblet gravy every single Thanksgiving.

Some relatives are like bunions. They refuse to go away, and you can't get rid of them without a chainsaw.

And it's not just family feuds either. Friendly fire is equally destructive when we're hurt by another Christian, church leadership, or someone we consider a friend. Even our spouse. These sniper attacks are triply damaging because they rupture trust, faith, and love, the cords that bind personal relationships together. Like a frayed rope, the relationship, once it begins unraveling, is awfully hard to stop.

Feels like sheer torture, doesn't it, when we know we need to forgive someone we can't avoid who has hurt us—intentionally or unintentionally—but we just can't get past the resentment? The anger. The injustice.

Something that's helped me immensely with friendly fire forgiveness is a concept found in James 2:13: mercy trumps justice. Justice has its place in God's hierarchy of principles, certainly, but mercy is at the tip top of the list. Let me say it again because this is huge: mercy trumps justice. In Spades, my favorite card game, mercy would be the ace of spades; it trumps every other card in the deck. You play the mercy card and you win the trick. Period.

Mercy is all powerful, all dominating, all victorious.

As important as justice feels to us when we've been unjustly treated, it's not the trump card. Mercy is far more important to Papa God than justice (or its first cousin, revenge) and exponentially more valuable to the condition of our souls. "There will be no mercy for you if you have not shown mercy to others. But if you have been merciful, God will be merciful when he judges you" (James 2:13 NLT).

Another biblical rule of thumb that's helped me successfully execute friendly fire forgiveness is this: love the sinner, hate the sin. Yes, that's really in the Bible, but not in those exact words. "Be tender with sinners, but not soft on sin. The sin itself stinks to high heaven" (Jude 1:23 MSG). Separating the hurtful action from the person performing it somehow makes forgiveness easier. In your mind, the offense becomes an inanimate object that can be discarded and forgotten, rather than an inseparable, integral part of the offender's personality that looms indefinitely over your head like a dangling grenade.

It also helps to flip the friendly fire forgiveness coin. Look at it from another herspective. I certainly hope the folks I've hurt over the years won't define me by my bad behavior. I look back on some of my horrid insensitivities and cringe. It's my heartfelt prayer that they won't hold the nasty things I've said, hurtful things I've done, or stupid oversights I've made against me for the rest of my life. I'm more than a list of my past mistakes. Jesus made sure of that.

I desperately hope those I've offended will find the mercy necessary to love the sinner while hating the sin and allow me the freedom of starting afresh in our relationship after the slate's been wiped clean by forgiveness.

How, then, could I offer any less to those who've offended me?

FORGIVING WHEN IT HURTS

My friend Caryl (same gal from chapter 13) is an awesome example of forgiving when it's dreadfully hard. Caryl and her husband sold their home to people who moved in but never made payments and destroyed nearly everything in the house before disappearing. The financial liability fell back on Caryl and her husband, who were unable to cover the enormous bills and were soon forced into bankruptcy.

Forgiveness did not come easy. These people caused deep hurt. They'd carelessly inflicted damage that would continue to cause Caryl's family major financial problems and humiliation for many years to come. The normal human response would be resentment and bitterness. And maybe a little lust for retribution. Perfectly understandable, right?

But Caryl knew that her responsibility as a believer was to forgive. Even when the offender didn't ask for it. Even when they didn't deserve it. Even though she didn't particularly want to forgive.

You know, sometimes we hang on to unforgiveness like a tattered old elastically challenged bra. Although that droopy thing has lost all semblance of support and allows our bosom buddies to sag to our navels, we've gotten used to it and keep flopping around in it because it's easier than shelling out forty bucks and breaking in a new one. We don't realize how beautifully things could be looking up and take on a whole new perky attitude if we only got rid of that ugly, ineffective garment and donned a new one.

"Forgiveness is not a feeling," Caryl says. "It's an act of obedience to God. It's not pretending you weren't hurt; it doesn't condone what they did. It's deciding to not hold it against them any longer. Forgiveness is freeing. It releases you. It released me."

That freedom. . .that release Caryl speaks of is real, you know. It's the fabulous spiritual byproduct of forgiving someone. The prisoner set free is you.

Did you know that as a Christian, reconciliation is your ministry? To reconcile means to resolve differences, to restore harmony. That's forgiveness in a nutshell. And it's the assignment Papa God has personally given each believer. "God. . .reconciled us to himself through Christ and gave us the ministry of reconciliation" (2 Corinthians 5:18 NIV).

So the next time you think forgiving that atrocious person—in my case, a two-year-old bully the size of a stuffed panda—is simply beyond your capabilities, remember that forgiveness is not just a request. Or a suggestion. Or simply a nice thing to do. It's your ministry. . .your spiritual job.

And the Master Builder will equip you with the tools you need to complete any job He assigns you. If Papa asks you to build a shed, He'll provide the hammer and nails. He has a designer spiritual toolbox all ready and waiting for you.

People, even more than things, have to be restored, renewed,
revived, reclaimed, and redeemed; never throw out anyone.

~Audrey Hepburn

FOLLOWING MY PERSONAL GPS
(GOD-POWERED SATELLITE)

1. Have you had any run-ins lately with a two-year-old (or someone who acted like one) whom you had a hard time forgiving? What happened?

2. We've all been wounded by friendly fire at one time or another. Who was/is your worst sniper? Have you been able to forgive this person?

3. How can the concept "mercy trumps justice" help you gain a different herspective of a specific injustice you've suffered?

4. How does "Love the sinner; hate the sin" apply to your life at the moment?

5. Let's close this chapter on forgiveness with a wonderful message from Papa: "For God was in Christ, reconciling the world to himself, no longer counting people's sins against them. And he gave us this wonderful message of reconciliation" (2 Corinthians 5:19 NLT). Can you think of one way you can share this wonderful message of forgiveness with others this week?

SECTION 4

The Destination Is My Journey

You are a gracious and compassionate God, slow to anger and abounding in love.
JONAH 4:2 NIV

CHAPTER 19

Even the Brightest Sheen Won't Disguise a Clunker
(Inside-Out Love)

Three things will last forever—faith, hope, and love—and the greatest of these is love.
1 CORINTHIANS 13:13 NLT

||||||||||||||||||||||||||||||||||||||||||||||||||||||||||||||||||||||||||||||||||||||||||||||||||||||||||||||||||||||||||||||||||||||||||||||||||

I paused in my presentation to quickly scan my audience. They were a group of men and women from a church denomination rumored to be the "frozen chosen." Yep, I thought, a pretty accurate description. I've seen frozen turkeys more animated.

The kicker is, I'm an inspirational speaker who's known for sharing "truth gift-wrapped in humor," so one of the main reasons I'm invited to speak is to draw a smile from my audience. Maybe even a chuckle or a guffaw. Occasionally a profound belly laugh.

But nothing was happening here. A profusion of nothing, actually. One lady in the back almost showed her teeth. Once. But maybe that was a grimace. Or a hot flash. When I finished my most hilarious story, I think I might have heard a single snicker. Or it could've been a snort.

I felt like I was rolling around the toilet bowl in a slow flush, about to disappear down the black hole of no return.

I had to remind myself that I couldn't really know what these people were feeling inside, although on the outside their collective body language screamed "catatonic." They did seem to be loosening up a smidge as I kept hacking away at the granite that was their faces, and by the end, I actually counted seven teeth and a partial plate.

At that point, I was happy with crumbs.

To my amazement, as the fine, fastidious folks filed by my book table on their way out, nearly all of them bought books and thanked me for coming. I couldn't believe how many times someone stood before me with an expression that looked like their dog just died and said something to the effect of, "Wow. That was wonderful. I haven't laughed that hard in a long time."

Really?

Go figure.

Life's like that, isn't it? We never really know the effect we're having on other people. . .how much of us is rubbing off on our family, friends, coworkers, neighbors. They don't necessarily show it, but they're internalizing bits and pieces of us all the time. Just like we are of them. Little pieces that fit together like a puzzle to make us who we end up being in this life.

If we're acting as Papa God's hands and feet on earth, many of those bits and pieces are the byproduct of His limitless love passing through us into them. By serving others, we're loving them from the inside out. "Through love serve one another" (Galatians 5:13 NKJV).

And hear this: they're feeling that love at some level, whether they acknowledge it or not.

NOTHING SAYS "I LOVE YOU"
LIKE FRYING BACON

As a confused teenager searching for something elusive that I couldn't seem to find (a nice way of saying this was my nasty phase), I went through a period of coldness toward my mother. I simply could not bring myself to admit my love for her or acknowledge hers for me.

When she would say, "I love you" in the evening before bed, I'd mutely close my bedroom door in her face. As I passed through the kitchen where she was cooking dinner after a long workday, she would often reach out, wrap her weary arms around me, and declare, "I love you so much!" My reply was to stand as stiff and unresponsive as a marble statue. To my utmost shame, I recall breaking her embrace and pushing her away more than once.

Yet she never gave up on me. She continued to tell me day after week after month how much she loved me, not only verbally but in acts of service, too. Like doing my laundry, taking the wimpy chicken wing from the platter so the meaty leg was left for me, and getting up early every morning to prepare my sister and me a hearty breakfast before school.

Ah, nothing says love quite like the smell of crispy fried bacon and hot buttered french toast with maple syrup.

For more than a year, Mama continued to love me while receiving squat in return. Not only did I not respond in a positive way to her selfless, unconditional love, but it also appeared that I couldn't have cared less. But I did care. And I did receive her love down deep inside, where it nurtured a spark that in time grew into a blaze that gradually thawed my frigid heart.

Isn't that the same way we resist Papa God's love at times? Especially when we've done something we feel guilty about and think we don't deserve His all-forgiving, all-accepting love.

Perhaps our resistance is because of shame. Or possibly unresolved anger. Whatever the reason, we stiffen up like unresponsive marble statues and maybe even push Him away. Yet He never gives up on us. He just keeps on wrapping His big, comforting arms around us and loving us anyway.

That's agape, baby.

My mom's human example of Papa God's superhuman love has given me the motivation to be patient with my own teens and others in my life who don't appear to return my love. To use an analogy all women understand, you just never know how long it'll take all those separate ingredients boiling together to thicken into fudge.

KINDNESS: SILENT LOVE

No, outsides may not reflect insides. Things aren't always what they seem. Sometimes we end up being immensely blessed because they're not. Like the warm relationship my mother and I share today despite all the times I acted like a cold carp. And like a man named Ron's finale. . .that wasn't.

Poor Ron, a former teacher, couldn't stop coughing. After many inconclusive medical tests, X-rays turned up a dark spot on his lung. As he anxiously awaited word from physicians on what they'd found during exploratory surgery, the dreaded C-word hovered over his head like an ominous storm cloud. All signs pointed that direction. What else could it be?

Well, does the term *pea sprout* come to mind? No kidding. Somehow Ron had sucked a pea he was eating down the wrong pipe (what we belles call aspiration), and it ended up embedding itself in the lining of his lung. Didn't take long for the wayward pea to sprout in the warm, moist environment and cause a dickens of a problem. Not exactly the best place for a summer garden.

Ron was not convinced it wasn't cancer until the pathology report came back: vegetable.[14]

We can all be full of surprises. Maybe not surprises like gut-grown pea patches, but if we have Papa's agape love filling our lives to the brim so that it spills over onto those around us (remember 1 Thessalonians 3:12 from chapter 12), we can certainly surprise ourselves and others with unexpected gestures of kindness. I like to call it silent love.

My friend Derek told me of a wonderful example of kindness. A woman came in the South Carolina car repair shop where Derek worked. She was a single mother with a young child and badly needed all four tires replaced on her car but could only afford two. As she sat in the waiting room entertaining her toddler while Derek worked on her car, another customer approached him and asked how much two additional tires would cost. The man paid for her tires and left.

Derek was deeply moved when the work was completed and he saw the effect of the stranger's kindness on that young woman. Her grateful tears touched his heart, and you can bet neither Derek nor any of his customers that day will ever forget the silent love demonstrated by that selfless man who sought no acknowledgment for his deed of kindness.

Then there was the amazing exchange of kindness between complete strangers that took place in Wisconsin one crisp fall Saturday in 2011. Victor, a sixty-one-year-old man, stopped on the side of a busy interstate to help a young nursing assistant named Ann and her cousin Lisa change a blown tire. Victor's wife comforted Ann and Lisa like she would have her own daughters during the fifteen minutes Victor took to change the tire as cars barreled by. Then they all said their good-byes like old friends and went on their way.

Victor eased his pickup back onto the highway while Ann and Lisa tarried awhile to decom-stress and talk about how thankful they were for the unexpected help.

Several miles down the highway, the girls were surprised to come upon Victor's pickup on the shoulder of the road, his wife standing beside it frantically waving her arms. Ann immediately pulled over to find that shortly after they'd reentered the traffic flow, Victor had gone into sudden cardiac arrest and his wife had to lean over and steer the car off the busy interstate. Ann administered CPR until EMS arrived. She was credited with saving Victor's life.

"I one hundred percent believe God put Lisa and me and those people in the right place at the right time," Ann said. "I'm so grateful for that."[15]

We'll talk more about kindness—silent love—in chapter 23, but for now suffice it to say that without Papa's inside-out love, our efforts fall short. We can do nice things for people all day, but if we're not doing them out of agape love, our outsides may look pretty impressive but our insides are hollow. A clunker with a shine. We're like a beautifully polished red Porsche chassis with no engine beneath the hood. An empty Gucci shoe box. A lovely, shiny, silver Christmas bell that doesn't tinkle merrily but instead clangs like an annoying gong.

Does that last one sound familiar? It should if you've read 1 Corinthians 13:

> *"What if I could speak all languages of humans and of angels?*
> *If I did not love others, I would be nothing more*
> *than a noisy gong or a clanging cymbal. . .*
> *What if I had faith that moved mountains?*
> *I would be nothing unless I loved others.*
> *What if I gave away all that I owned. . .*
> *I would gain nothing unless I loved others."*
> (1 Corinthians 13:1–3 CEV)

Love. We can either embrace it or disgrace it.

It's not about all the good deeds we can do, the money we can donate, the homeless we can feed. It's not *what* we do, it's *why*. Because when our inside-out focus reverses to outside-in, we lose sight of our upward purpose and fall into a downward spiral. Without loving like Papa as our motivation and goal, we begin to clang and gong, irritate and chafe.

Christ-servers don't do things for others because of what we can get in return. We do them to spread Papa's eternal love to others. To love others into His warm, welcoming arms so they can experience His incredible, never-ending agape love, too.

How do we come up with that type of love-with-no-strings-attached motivation? Well, it begins inside us. When we finally comprehend Papa God's unswerving, extravagant, and intimate love for us, from our toenails to our split ends, then our hearts will begin to overflow with His boundary-less love from our inside out. It's only then that we can truly serve our brothers and sisters the way our heavenly Father intended us to. . .in a spirit of love.

Then one day, before the show's over, maybe we'll take the opportunity to tell those with whom we've exchanged life puzzle pieces how much a part of us they really are. How much they've meant to us. How we've honestly been blessed by them, although we might not have shown it by our granite faces.

We can then slap one another on the back and say, "Wow. That was wonderful. I haven't loved that hard in a long time."

To find someone who will love you for no reason, and to shower that person with reasons, that is the ultimate happiness.

~ROBERT BRAULT

FOLLOWING MY PERSONAL GPS (GOD-POWERED SATELLITE)

1. Can you recall a time in your life when you resisted Papa God's love? Why?

2. How about a time when a cold carp (hardened person) didn't respond to your demonstrations of love or kindness? How did you deal with it?

3. As you probably know by now, yummy food shouts love to me (give me Cadbury with almonds and I'll be your BFF for all eternity). Now think a minute—is there someone in your life who speaks love to you not by words but by actions? How do these actions meet a need of yours or make you feel special? Have you ever acknowledged that you've received those actions as evidence of silent love?

4. How do you show love to others by your actions? Read aloud 1 Corinthians 13:1–3 (page 177). Think of one person in your life to whom you could demonstrate your love better. How might you do that?

5. Would you consider yourself a kind person? Someone who regularly shows others the Lord's inside-out silent love overflowing from your heart? Why or why not? How do you think you might become a kinder version of your current self?

CHAPTER 20

Sphincter-Pucker Moments
(Curbing Anxiety)

How priceless is your unfailing love, O God!
People take refuge in the shadow of your wings.
PSALM 36:7 NIV

The day before my friend Cheryl was scheduled to finish paying off her first car, a perky little Sunbird, she offered a college friend, Gwen, a ride home. The two young women had just turned out of the university parking lot when they heard sirens growing louder.

Cheryl glanced in her rearview mirror and was shocked to see a souped-up Mustang barreling up behind her with a police car in hot pursuit. Before she could do more than gulp, the Mustang plowed into the back of her Sunbird at high speed, buckling the trunk onto the rear wheels. The girls screamed as the car lurched forward.

The Mustang shoved the Sunbird into the curb, where it became airborne before landing 120 feet away. The driver of the Mustang, which crashed right behind Cheryl's car, took off running but was tackled by a cop. Turned out he was majorly high on drugs and before he'd demolished Cheryl's car, had killed a bicyclist, nearly severed the leg of a motorcyclist, and smashed into a car full of little girls on their way to Brownies.

Mama mia. Feeling a little anxious while reading this? I know I am while writing it. That's because we're both well acquainted with those anxiety-producing, sphincter-pucker moments in our own lives.

Well, by the grace of God, Cheryl and Gwen were miraculously okay, although Gwen smashed the windshield with her shoulder and everything around Cheryl was crunched. . .the dashboard, steering wheel, even Cheryl's solid gold bangle was mangled. Everything was broken except Cheryl. The girls walked away unscathed except for a few scrapes and bruises.

My heart's still jumpy just picturing the twisted aftermath of one person's horrendous choices, isn't yours?

Anxiety about becoming injured or debilitated is very real to many of us. In fact, it ranks in the top ten fears women struggle with in the survey of five hundred women I conducted while preparing to write *Fear, Faith, and a Fistful of Chocolate*. (Bet you'll recognize many of the other fears discussed in that book as your own—I certainly do!)

Most of us experience anxiety on an everyday basis in just coping with the myriad of challenges twenty-first-century womanhood thrusts on us—making split-second decisions, beating ridiculous deadlines, herding wildebeest children, encouraging beaten-down husbands, stretching dollars like rubber bands, and processing constant interruptions.

I believe much of the anxiety we experience is due to insecurity— insecurity based on a deeper fear of loss. We blanch at the possibility of losing any number of things important to us—independence, respect, health, or possessions to name a few.

But most of all, we fear losing love. Being left all alone. Deserted by God and man.

LEADING LADYBIRD

One morning on my prayer walk with my dog Fenway (can you guess what baseball logo graces most of Spouse's boxers?),

I happened upon a pair of cardinals shopping for a nice grass seed breakfast. They were so busy pecking the ground they didn't notice Fenway straining on his leash for enough leeway to get up close and personal with the new couple on the block.

The little mister, in his gorgeous flaming crimson suit, became aware of us first. He skittered a bit closer to the female, in her much more subdued red plumage (sort of like a faded housecoat). But she was too preoccupied with her shopping list to notice. I totally get that. To-do lists are all consuming in any species. When she still didn't look up as he hopped about in a distressed little "Hey, Edna, pay attention, will ya?" circle, he just up and flew away.

What? Where'd the little twit go? What a cowardly thing to do. Desert your woman at the first hint of trouble. Save yourself. Don't hang around to help her; just go off to do your own thing. Humph. My fist landed on my hip, my eyebrows trespassed into my hairline, and my head started twitching in the standard womanly "You've *got* to be kidding me!" gesture (you know, the one you usually reserve for nature trail litterers and rebellious teens sneaking in after curfew).

I was hugely indignant on Ladybird's behalf. Yet she kept her beak to the grindstone. She kept on pecking away at her chores, oblivious to the potential danger not ten feet away.

I found myself channeling to my feathered sister, *You deserve better than him, honey. He's throwing you to the dogs. Good riddance to the jerk!*

Suddenly the missing mister bellowed a piercing chirp so loud it startled the bejeebies out of Fenway and me.

Ladybird immediately looked upward to where her fella sat perched on a branch high above the fray and flew directly to his side. I can only surmise he had squawked something along the lines of, "Edna, get your tail feathers up here *right now!*"

Once she was safely beside him on the overhead branch, he leaned over and tapped her beak with his very, very gently— almost like a tender kiss—and together they gazed down at my furry four-legged buddy and me gawking up at them. My self-righteous 'tude came unglued.

Oh. Oops. My bad.

Apparently, I was mistaken. He wasn't leaving her. He was *leading* her. The same way Spouse sometimes leads me when I won't listen the first time he makes a good suggestion. The way Papa God leads me when I'm too busy trying to accomplish my to-do list to pay attention to His still, small voice.

As Fenway and I left the lovebirds and moved on down the block, I had a God-smack moment, as my friend Gil calls those flashes of sudden enlightenment. It struck me that I had jumped to the abandonment conclusion awfully quickly. But why? Why had I immediately assumed that was the case and gotten so hot about it?

Hmm. Could it possibly be because I secretly fear that I, too, may one day be abandoned? Not just by my mate, but by my Lord? In my heart of hearts, I knew it was true. I can live without many things, but not without love.

PAPA'S NOT LETTING GO

One of mankind's oldest and strongest emotions is fear of losing God's love. Adam and Eve demonstrated that fear by their hide-and-please-don't-seek game with their Creator after they'd sinned in the garden of Eden (I told the Deb version of this Genesis story in chapter 14). Indeed, that type of fear has been around a long time—the faulty notion that we can do something bad enough to ultimately destroy our heavenly Father's divine devotion. That we can, by our stupid, reprehensible behavior, permanently dissolve our relationship with our Redeemer (as He is referred to in Isaiah 59:20).

But we have one crucial consolation: the only emotion older

and stronger than fear is love. We cannot break that bond of love our Creator has with us no matter what we do. The bond may be damaged by our reckless disregard for His standards, but He promises the connection will never be completely severed.

And where even one sliver of thread remains, restoration is possible.

He truly is our Redeemer, which means "One who repairs or restores." Yahweh loved Adam and Eve before and after they'd sinned. Sure, He was disappointed and upset with them because of their disobedience (like we are when our children disobey us and make a terrible mistake).

But He still loved them.

Regardless of their actions, He loved them. Relentlessly. Redeemingly.

And He will always love us. Regardless of our actions. He knows our bad behavior doesn't define who we are. He knows better than anyone who we really are—the woman He created us to be. The core of our being was known to Him and already well loved at the beginning of time. "Even before he made the world, God loved us and chose us in Christ" (Ephesians 1:4 NLT). How did He do that? It's one of those wonderful and mysterious facts of faith.

But still we worry that we'll not make the cut.

Listen, there's only one unpardonable sin, found in Luke 12:10: "If you bad-mouth the Son of Man [Jesus] out of misunderstanding or ignorance, that can be overlooked. But if you're knowingly attacking God himself, taking aim at the Holy Spirit, that won't be overlooked" (MSG). Thankfully, those of us who love our mighty God and have accepted Jesus as our Savior will never have to worry about intentionally blaspheming the Holy Spirit. Everything else is forgivable. Everything. "If we confess our sins to him, he is faithful and just to forgive us our sins and to cleanse us from all wickedness" (1 John 1:9 NLT).

Did you notice that terribly important word, every? *Every* wrong. Papa will never stop forgiving and forgetting our screwups. "How far has the LORD taken our sins from us? Farther than the distance from east to west!" (Psalm 103:12 CEV).

SNUG AND SAFE AND WARM

So we don't have to live in fear of Him deserting us in disgust or disappointment. Our Papa God promises that we'll always find safety, refuge, and peace in the shadow of His wings, like we've already seen in Psalm 36:7 at the beginning of this chapter. Read it again and savor the words *priceless. . .unfailing. . .refuge.*

I just love that imagery of a loving, protective momma bird drawing her young in close during a gathering storm and covering them with her wings, the strongest part of her body. Nothing can harm her precious babes without getting through her first. She's ready to sacrifice her life for them if necessary.

There are other scriptures that refer to us finding protection in the shadow of Papa God's wings. I encourage you to look them up in your Bible and read the entire chapter containing each; none is very long. Write out the verses below as your personal prayer; they're wonderful outpourings of trust in the One who has already sacrificed everything on a brutal cross to protect you from harm.

❋ Psalm 17:8

❋ Psalm 57:1

❋ Psalm 61:4

❀ Psalm 91:4

And my personal fave, a passage that has helped me through many an anxiety-ridden night, is Psalm 63:6–7: "On my bed I remember you; I think of you through the watches of the night. Because you are my help, I sing in the shadow of your wings" (NIV).

Incredibly beautiful, isn't it? Because we can find protection and abiding peace in the shadow of the strong, warm wings hovering over us, we're able to rejoice by bursting forth with song and praise, even as the wildest storm pounds on the outside of our cozy little nest. We can relax in complete security, knowing that our ever-loving Lord has us covered.

PEACE, CUSTOM-GIFTED TO YOU WITH LOVE

Okay, girlfriend, let's uncoil. Chill. Feel the peace.

But hanging on to that peace in our mad-stressful world often feels elusive, doesn't it? Especially in relationships. Peace seems hard to grasp and even harder to hang on to. But we need to understand something important about peace. It's not merely the absence of conflict. It's deeper than that. Peace is more than just a cease-fire, a temporary cessation of bombardment.

Peace is not a weapon of mass destruction; it's mass destruction of our weapons.

Authentic peace is a state of mind and heart, not an external condition like a cease-fire, a laying aside of aggression. The mutually agreed-upon truce that results from a cease-fire isn't really lasting peace; it's only a stopgap in hostilities. Vehemence is still there, only muted.

To put it in girl-speak, the foot hasn't changed, only the nail polish.

But in true peace—Papa's peace—the destructive feelings

have been obliterated. They no longer exist. They've been replaced by supernatural love. The whole foot has been renewed by His loving pedicure; ugly calluses have been filed down to smoothness, sharp nails sanded, dirty skin cleaned, softened, and scented.

How do we achieve this lovely supernatural makeover?

Genuine peace is entirely dependent on trust in God's sovereignty. That means believing He's in control of all the details of our lives, even if it doesn't feel like it. There's nothing random or accidental about acquiring peace. You don't stumble upon lasting peace because the sky is blue, the birds are singing, and you lost three pounds last week. The cornerstone to finding peace is making the decision to trust Papa God. No matter what.

Like the SAM guys did in the third chapter of Daniel. "Sam who?" you ask. It's an acronym for their names: Shadrach, Abednego, and Meshach. As you recall, they were three Israeli teens who were captured and transported as slaves to Babylon. Ordered by their new king to worship his idol god or die horribly in a fiery furnace, the boys evoked the SAM Creed: My God is able to deliver me, but even if He chooses not to, I will still follow Him.

When you and I evoke the SAM Creed, we're taking the biggest step possible toward inner peace. We're choosing to not yield to anxiety about our volatile, constantly changing circumstances but instead to trust that Papa is in control and whatever He chooses to do, we will still follow Him.

It's in adopting the SAM Creed as our own that we find peace.

One of my favorite verses about peace is John 14:27 (NLT): "I am leaving you with a gift—peace of mind and heart. And the peace I give is a gift the world cannot give. So don't be troubled or afraid." Nice. His gift to you is that supernatural pedicure we talked about earlier. Peace custom-gifted specifically to you with love by Yeshua, the Prince of Peace.

And did you recognize that His peace is completely different than the world's peace, with its superficial truces and cease-fires and Nobel Prizes? His peace is long and lasting and love-inspired. And it acts as a fear shield to our vulnerable minds and hearts. . . something we all desperately need.

I introduced my acronym for PEACE in *Too Blessed to Be Stressed*, and I think it's a good time to review it.

P: Placing
E: Each
A: Aggravation at
C: Christ's feet. . .
E: Expectantly!

Biblical peace is acquired by intentionally handing your heavenly Father your daily annoyances, dilemmas, and burdens one by one, minute by minute. By giving up the steering wheel. By making the choice to relax in the backseat and let Papa drive.

Only then will your senses come alive through His peace. Only then will you begin to feel the splendor of warm summer rain on your skin, see the beauty of dew-touched spiderwebs, smell the sweet aroma of blooming gardenias, and taste the Christmassy comfort of cinnamon. You'll know you are deeply loved by gazing at the sparkling light of a sunbeam filtering through leaves like Papa God's fingers reaching down to you from heaven.

Now that's peace, sister.

Peace smells like freshly baked chocolate chip cookies, soft, buttery, and warm from the oven. Sit back, taste, and know that the Master Baker should have his own cooking show.
~Debora M. Coty

FOLLOWING MY PERSONAL GPS (GOD-POWERED SATELLITE)

1. Recount a recent anxiety-producing sphincter-pucker moment you've gone through. How did you see the hand of Papa God protecting you?

2. What speaks to you most about the imagery of hiding in the shadow of Papa God's protective wings?

3. Is there anything in your past that makes it difficult for you to fully accept 1 John 1:9 (page 185)? Does guilt prevent you from recognizing forgiveness for *every* sin? If so, sister, you're not alone. What are some steps you can take to shed that guilt and embrace Psalm 103:12 (also on page 185)?

4. In which of your relationships do you find it hardest to achieve peace? Have you ever reached a cease-fire in that relationship? What's the difference? How can you progress from truce to biblical peace?

5. How does invoking the SAM Creed affect your level of personal inner peace?

CHAPTER 21

Hangin' with My Besties
(Feeding the Love)

Godly people are careful about the friends they choose.
PROVERBS 12:26 NIRV

||||||||||||||||||||||||||||||||||||||||||||||||||||||||||||||||||||||||||||||||||||||||||||||||||||||||||||||||||||||

Girlfriends. We need 'em, we love 'em, we can't jive without 'em. Like Anne of Green Gables, girls need bosom friends. Men are okay, but their bosoms just aren't the same. We need occasional silliness, moments of reckless feminine abandon, and a safe place to stash our secrets where they won't leak.

Girlfriends are the way we learn how to love unconditionally, just as our Godfriend loves us. "A friend loves at all times" (Proverbs 17:17 NIV). We learn to overlook zits, burps, and hideous hair days and honestly believe that this special person who hears the song down in our heart is the most beautiful creature on earth.

The very same way Papa views us.

Through loving our girlfriends, we learn forgiveness, compassion, mercy, and grace. Character traits straight from the heart of God. But to me, one of the most important things I gain from hangin' with my besties is laughter. Pure, soul-freeing, stress-dissolving belly laughter. I believe that laughter is the catalyst that releases the joy of the Lord in our souls, and nothing bubbles up joy like the hilarity of girlfriend giggles.

Ralph Waldo Emerson said, "It is the blessing of old friends that you can afford to be stupid with them." Amen, bro.

I like nothing better than getting together with the gals in my weekly neighborhood Bible study. It's always an adventure. We're a multiracial, multidenominational, multi-herspective bunch of varying ages. My soul sistahs and I seriously and earnestly dig in to God's Word and then seriously and earnestly dig in to delectables like chocolate-dipped strawberries, chicken salad croissants, and triple chunk brownies as we share learning, laughs, and life together. Occasional tears flow, true, but definitely lots of laughs.

From these and other educational chic chats, I've learned a few things—very important girl things—that I'd like to share with you now.

❀ An alligator clip on the tongue doesn't stymie blabber control issues.

❀ The best stress reliever women have is each other.

❀ You really don't want people to assume your hair stylist is from Oz.

❀ Life is what happens when we're waiting for it to start.

❀ I must rescue my own joy. . .because if I don't it will stay lost.

❀ Your punishment for trying to fix your mother is to turn into her.

❀ It's much more productive to be a warrior than a worrier.

❀ In my younger years, I just wanted to be "normal." Now I'm happy to be you-nique.

❀ Mothers have a way of becoming travel agents for a lifelong guilt trip.

❀ A woman over fifty stops growing at both ends and starts growing in the middle.

❀ When wearing your bathing suit on a beach, avoid eye contact with passing people—summer judging, summer not.

❀ Life is a long succession of frustrations, disappointments, and challenges, but eventually you will find a bra that fits.

❀ Quite often when the road looks like a dead end up ahead, it's really only a sharp turn. If you just stay on it a little longer, you'll find your way again.

❀ For a hundred-calorie snack you can choose between one large hard-boiled egg, two cups strawberry halves, seven Doritos, twenty-five baby carrots, two Reduced-Fat Oreos, one medium apple, or one cup of fresh blueberries. Tape this to your fridge. Save your calories for your next spat. Read on. . .

❀ Chocolate repairs relationship cracks. When an argument breaks out with your spouse or BFF, haul out your fave chocolate bar and share it. By the time you're finished, nerves are calmer, voices are lower, and you're both in a much more agreeable mood.

NEW NEAR-FACTS OF SCIENCE

Since I'm imparting feminine wit and near-wisdom, I mustn't neglect the new Coty Near-Facts of Science I've recently postulated (lots more are found sprinkled throughout my other books):

❀ Polite Calories: Sacrificial scarfing with the sole purpose of sparing someone's feelings. These calories don't count because you don't really want them, but you consume them just to be polite.

❀ The Michelin Man Syndrome: Gals over fifty tend to sprout a spare tire around the waist overnight. Also known as the dreaded jelly belly. Or the overflowing waist basket.

❀ The Flip-Flop Rule: Chocolate consumption is inversely proportionate to its application. For example, a quarter-pound of consumed Cadbury equals four pounds of thigh-u-lite; a half-pound of Ferrero Rocher equals two pounds additional Dumbo arm flap webbing.

❀ TIVI (pronounced, appropriately, TV): The unexplained phenomenon that renders males selectively blind to spills, stains, crumbs, or dirty socks on the floor.

  T: Testosterone
  I: Induced
  V: Vision
  I: Impairment

❀ And its cousin TIHI (pronounced tee-hee): The mysterious blockage of male auditory processing skills pertaining to specific phrases such as "Take out the trash" and "It's your turn to do the dishes."

  T: Testosterone
  I: Induced
  H: Hearing
  I: Impairment

Speaking of testosterone, my friend Jeanie says, "The only time my husband communicates with me is when he's snoring."

That rather jarring thought leads me to another Near-Fact of Science about the importance of communication in marriage. I call it: the You No Talk, You No Squawk Rule. The precept is that if there's no prior communication about an act performed in good faith (albeit with miserable results), you're not allowed to incessantly complain about it afterward.

I came to this painful conclusion after Spouse ever-so-helpfully snipped the top ten inches of growth off the poinsettias lining my front walkway. In mid-November. Just as they were about to transform into festive scarlet blooms for Christmas.

At first I thought it was the work of a despicable Christmas terrorist and wanted to call the police. "Oh, it was just me," Spouse said, carefree as a partridge in a pear tree as I fretted over my be-headed plants. "I thought they were getting too high so I trimmed them. How was I supposed to know those green leaves were the actual flowers?"

Sigh. I know. I really need to bury the man's gardening tools.

Now that I'm over fifty, regardless of how many hours I was up during the night (usually no small number), my internal rooster crows at 5:00 a.m. I wake up, slog out of bed, look in the mirror, and realize the new me is now the old me. Those Armani totes beneath my eyes remind me that sleep is overrated. I asked Papa God for more hours in the day, and He sent me menopause. Now I have half the stinkin' night, too.

My menopausal theme verse has become, "He awakens me morning by morning. He awakens my ear to listen as a disciple" (Isaiah 50:4–5 NASB).

Seriously, I used to grouse, grump, and gripe about being an unwilling early riser until I discovered this verse and recognized the privilege of being awakened by Papa God for those predawn hours with just the two of us while the rest of the world slumbers. Now I consider my intimate prayer-walks beneath the morning stars precious and priceless.

YAY-YAY FOR YA-YAS!

Okay, one last thought about the importance of Ya-Yas (as you already know, that's the term that became synonymous with girl-friend tribes after Sandra Bullock's delightful 2002 movie, *Divine Secrets of the Ya-Ya Sisterhood*). They're simply indispensable. No woman should live without Ya-Yas.

I belong to two tribes of Ya-Yas, one comprised of gals who've shared the same profession for decades, and the other, church friends who first met thirty years ago when we were, as my granny used to say, young and full of hope.

Tribe size doesn't matter; your sisterhood can have as few as four or as many as fifteen. The idea is to shed your beasties and bond with your besties during periodic outings like beach week-ends, mountain getaways, dinners out, sleepovers, Barry Manilow concerts (or better yet, Josh Groban—be still my heart!), and sub-lime chick flicks.

You know, things you can't drag your fella to and wouldn't really want to.

One of my Ya-Ya groups gets together twice yearly, the other quarterly. My friend Jan's Ya-Yas have been leaving their cares be-hind for girlfriend get-togethers for nearly twenty years. Jan cracks me up with tales of their zany adventures, like the overnight beach trip when everyone agreed to a hairdo-over. So they bought four-dollar color kits from Walmart and dyed one another's hair. They looked like a box of Crayola rejects. One poor gal's head went home strongly resembling a ripe banana; she had to spend over one hundred dollars on a repair job by a stylist.

Ya-Yas are the bosom friends that do the stuff of life with you; they walk every step of the way through illnesses, surgeries, marital woes, weddings, babies, deaths, personal tragedies, and triumphs. They understand you. They dry your tears with tears of their own. They laugh till the iced tea squirts out their nose. They totally get why you have a Winnie the Pooh cartoon taped to your microwave that says, "Do you ever stop to think and forget to start again?"

Your Ya-Yas sincerely believe you're a good egg even though you're hopelessly cracked. They start nodding their heads in agreement long before your last word crosses your lips. We need them. They need us.

United we stand; divided we go to the mall.

I'll never forget the time I was wallowing in the pit of despair after my third surgery within seven months (on the same knee) when my Ya-Yas appeared at my door equipped with perfume, makeup, pedicure supplies, and a delicious girlie luncheon just to cheer me up. By the time they left, I was break-dancing with my crutches.

Now that's Papa's love with toenail polish on it.

Friends are kisses blown to us by angels.
~UNKNOWN AUTHOR (but I wish it were me!)

🧭 FOLLOWING MY PERSONAL GPS (GOD-POWERED SATELLITE)

1. A kindred spirit once said, "A friend accepts us as we are but helps us to be better." In what way would you say this has been true in your experience?

2. Who would you consider your besties? What do you love about them?

3. According to Ecclesiastes 4:12 (MSG), "By yourself you're unprotected. With a friend you can face the worst." Can you recall a time when you were able to face the worst because of the love of a friend?

4. Do you belong to a tribe of Ya-Yas? Would you like to? How about starting one of your own? You'll be surprised how many gals are just as eager as you to belong to a sisterhood of love.

5. Which are your faves of my new Coty Near-Facts of Science on pages 192–193? I'd really be thrilled if you'd e-mail me your answer—I really love hearing from you!

CHAPTER 22

Papa God Specializes in Broken Heart Surgery
(Healing Hidden Hurts)

---✳---

He heals the brokenhearted and binds up their wounds.
Psalm 147:3 nasb

As I pedaled my bike down the quiet country road on my regular Sunday afternoon exercise trek, something I saw on the side of the road made me stop cold. I hadn't noticed it in a very long time, and on this particular day, its image of stark loneliness struck me as immeasurably sad.

It was a mighty oak, the trunk several feet in diameter and as tall as a three-story building. The tree had matured during the twenty years since I'd first laid eyes on it, back when it was a lanky teenage sapling and so terribly in love. Oh yeah, completely smitten and unafraid to show it.

You see, the oak had sprouted right beside a young palm tree, and the two had grown together, intertwined as it seemed, for all eternity. The oak had enveloped the palm's trunk base, surrounding it so that the palm seemed to spring from its very core. And then, as if to ensure a lifetime of intimacy, the oak had wrapped two small branches around the palm's trunk, with fingerlike twigs extending from the ends of clinging branches that looked exactly like arms embracing a lover.

Honestly, no woman with an ounce of romance in her soul could pass this tender scene without an *awww* escaping her lips. Love was their destiny, and it was a beautiful, stirring thing.

I always intended to snap a picture of this extraordinary arborous couple, but I kept putting it off.

And then one day it was too late. The palm tree was gone, severed from the arms that surrounded it with such devotion. The new property owners must have thought two trees growing in such proximity would eventually threaten the health of both, so they'd left the oak and chainsawed the palm away.

The poor, pathetic oak stood there with its arms frozen in an empty embrace, encircling, loving, protecting. . .nothing but air. My heart felt skewered every time I saw it, so in the passing years, I'd disciplined myself from looking in that direction.

Until this particular day. Would you believe it? After two long decades, that oak still had its arms locked in the same empty embrace. The hole in its center had never filled in, leaving the long-gone palm's imprint as if it were still there. Still adored. Still mourned. Still profoundly missed.

HIDDEN HURTS

You can identify with that oak, can't you? Perhaps it's not a lover who's been ripped from your embrace, but you completely comprehend deep, aching, persistent heartbreak. Maybe it's due to the excruciating loss of a parent, sibling, friend, special teacher, close relative, or—heaven forbid—a child. Your broken heart may be the result of wounds inflicted by careless people or residual scar tissue from shattered dreams, disillusionment, or disappointment.

Hidden hurts can be just as agonizing as physical injuries. And they often linger much, much longer.

Correct me if I'm wrong, but sometimes to avoid resolved pain, I suspect you find yourself simply turning off your feelings. You go through the motions of life, but you feel nothing. No highs. No lows. No elation. No sorrow. Your reasoning? Numbness is tolerable. Prolonged anguish is not.

I *so* get you, sister.

But author J. K. Rowling was right when she said, "Numbing the pain for a while will make it worse when you finally feel it." And at some point we must inevitably face that raw, unresolved pain that fractures our hearts and spirits.

All of us feel brokenness at one time or another. The good news is that Papa God loves us just the way we are—broken. But He also loves us enough not to leave us that way.

Did you know there are over 120 references in the New Testament alone of Jesus' healing mercies? That's great news for us, girlfriend; He really does perform broken heart surgery!

PREP FOR BROKEN HEART SURGERY

I've spoken candidly about my own periods of brokenness in my other books, so I won't repeat myself here, but I'd like to share some things I've found extremely helpful in propelling me onto Papa's operating table where His healing sutures sewed the tattered pieces back together.

❀ Develop soul sisters. Like I mentioned in the last chapter, hang with girls willing to connect with you spiritually— study the Bible, pray together, point each other toward Jesus. They're the best healing ointment there is.

❀ Make a play date with yourself. Yep, you heard me right. I'm giving you permission to cut loose. Relaxing and having fun are important to the emotional healing process. Do an activity you enjoyed as a child; try something new with a friend. Enjoy emotional refreshment through the rejuvenating power of laughter. Cast off your cares, and allow your spirit to float for a few hours.

❀ Spend time alone with Papa God. Carve out at least fifteen minutes of one-on-one face time daily to talk with and listen to Him. Prayer walks are great for this. Pour out your heartache. Then listen with your spiritual ears. Be still, and know He is God. Don't tie Him to a chair in the basement of your life. Make space in your day for Him to move.

❀ Work through your crisis of faith. I call it the Dungeon of Doubt. Don't stay chained in the blackness of that hopeless pit. You have a key and a ladder. The key is Papa's promise to never leave you or forsake you; the ladder is His strength to climb out one rung at a time. You may have to feel around the dark dungeon until you find them.

Doubting our faith is natural when we're in the throes of heartbreak. One of my own experiences in the Dungeon of Doubt is chronicled in chapter 12 of *More Beauty, Less Beast*. We all feel doubt at one time or another, but please hear this: you mustn't stay in your dungeon, sister, even though at the moment you might feel too sucked dry to attempt the first rung on the arduous climb.

Perhaps you blame yourself. . .or someone else for your dungeon imprisonment. Or maybe you blame God. Many people do. In fact, I'd venture to say 98 percent of us do during a crisis of faith; that's why we're wracked with doubt. We want to trust. We want to believe. But we can't get over the pain. And deep down we're angry that Papa could have prevented our brokenness but didn't.

I learned something from *Forrest Gump*'s Lieutenant Dan that's echoed in wise counsel from many Christian pastors and counselors: you'll never escape your Dungeon of Doubt until you duke it out with God. Remember how Lt. Dan climbed the shrimp boat's mast and screamed his rage and defiance toward the Almighty in the wild winds of the hurricane?

Old Testament Jacob did it, too. He not only emotionally duked it out, but he also engaged in actual physical combat with Yahweh and ended up with a lifelong hitch in his get-along to prove it. The Genesis 32 account of Jacob's Almighty wrestling match reassures us that the Lord is not offended when we beat on His chest and shout, "Why?" He understands that we must sometimes wrestle out the mysteries of our faith. Confronting his Master was the turning point for Jacob—he got a new name (Israel) and a new lease on life.

Papa is ready to do the same for us. We, too, need to confront Jehovah with our pain, frustration, and heartbreak before we can find our personal peace with Him and move on.

In order for Papa God to mend a broken heart, He needs all the fragments; it's up to us to give Him each and every stained, chipped, flawed shard.

Listen, it's really okay. You can yell and cry and shake your fist. He's a very big God. He can take your ballistic tirade. And then He'll lovingly envelop you in His warmth, comfort, and reassurance. That marvelous peace that surpasses all understanding will eventually reconnect your heart and your mind with Christ Jesus (Ephesians 4:7). But be patient—you may have to spend some time in Papa's waiting room in the meantime. I know I did.

❀ Obey what Papa God instructs you to do. Even if it doesn't make sense. Obedience opens the door for miracles.

Biblical examples of seemingly crazy obedience abound: The Red Sea parted when Moses obeyed Yahweh's directive to raise a stick in the air (Exodus 14:16–21). The enormous stone walls of Jericho crumbled into rubble when the Creator of the Universe told Joshua and his men to toot a horn (Joshua 6:1–20). Peter walked on water when he obeyed Jesus' simple call to "Come" (Matthew 14:25–33). Although the command must have seemed ludicrous, the paralyzed man (who likely had been bedridden for decades) scrambled to his feet when Jesus said, "Rise and walk" (Matthew 9:2–7). Even a dead man received the ultimate healing when he obeyed Jesus' command, "Lazarus, come forth!" (John 11:38–44).

Liberated from the grave, Lazarus literally became a dead man walking.

And that's pretty much what I felt like when, out of sheer obedience, I began using the "screaming at God" Psalms as my means of communication when I couldn't muster up a single prayer from my Dungeon of Doubt. Eventually (it took two years), my obedience in staying in the Word despite my disillusionment resulted in the miracle of healing and reconciliation with my Savior.

❀ Believe in Papa's power and His desire to heal you. You don't have to understand all the hows, whens, and whys; you just need faith. Do you recall the definition of faith? "Faith is confidence in what we hope for and assurance about what we do not see" (Hebrews 11:1 NIV).

Once, while I was hiking a mountain trail, I heard the stout gurgle of a flowing stream, but I couldn't see the water anywhere. I followed the sound to a leaf covered embankment. The stream wasn't visible, but nevertheless it was there, flowing beneath the thick layer of forest debris waiting to offer life sustenance and refreshment.

So much like faith. A life-enriching, joy-producing stream of supernatural strength flows beneath the concealing heartaches of life. But it's useless unless we believe it's there and look for it. St. Augustine said, "Understanding is the reward given by faith. Do not try to understand in order to believe, but believe in order to understand."

PERSEVERANCE FOR PRODIGAL CHILDREN

Mothers of prodigal children are indivisibly acquainted with dependence on faith without the benefit of understanding. They live with so many unanswered questions: How did this happen? Did I cause my child to stray? Why doesn't God do something?

These heartbroken women feel like love's hostages. As my friend Joy says, "When they're little, children step on your toes. When they're older, they step on your heart."

Elise is a BFF (Blessed Friend Forever) of mine who was heartbroken for years over her prodigal daughter, Belinda. Although she was raised in a godly home and was active in church growing up, Belinda rebelled as soon as she graduated, moving far away to engage in a hedonistic lifestyle that made Elise mourn.

For years, through endless tears, Elise prayed for Papa God to do whatever He must to bring Belinda back to faith in Jesus, even if it took personal tragedy to get Belinda's attention. Elise surely didn't want harm to come to her daughter, but she felt that if it was necessary to bring Belinda back to her spiritual senses, it was worth it.

Then one day a godly friend shared two herspective-altering scriptures with Elise. The first was Proverbs 22:6 (NIV): "Start children off on the way they should go, and even when they are old they will not turn from it." What a hope-filled promise!

The second was Romans 2:4 (NLT): "Don't you see how wonderfully kind, tolerant, and patient God is with you? Does this mean nothing to you? Can't you see that his kindness is intended to turn you from your sin?" The friend suggested that instead of praying for the Lord to jerk Belinda to her senses by something cataclysmic, Elise should pray for His kindness, tolerance, and patience to lead Belinda toward repentance. That Papa would bless Belinda so dramatically, she couldn't help but see His hand in it.

And do you know that's exactly what happened? Through a series of mini-miracles that (as Elise pointed out to her) could have only been from Papa God, Belinda's spiritual eyes were opened to His all-forgiving, never-ending love, and her life began transforming. She is now in the process of returning to her spiritual roots and has become a dedicated wife and mother of two beautiful children who are developing a strong faith in Jesus.

If you're the parent of a prodigal child, I encourage you to lean on these two passages in your hopes, dreams, and prayers. Persist as a stump mother.

"Um. . .what's a stump mother?" you ask. Well, I'll tell you.

I've been longtime prayer partners with two women (in addition to Elise) whose love has lain bruised and bleeding for many years over children who've turned away from their first love—Jesus—and continue to make poor choices throughout their teen and young adult years. Those poor choices resulted in ongoing lifestyles of apathy and disregard toward things of God.

Both women feel like complete failures as Christian mothers. Yet I eyewitnessed these selfless, dedicated, and supremely loving moms striving to plant Jesus' love deep in the hearts of their children. From the day they were born, these kids' days were filled with good things, healthy things, both spiritually and physically

. . .Christian music, scripture, creativity, caring people, art, beauty, fun. Under their mothers' loving supervision, each one blossomed with the talents and gifts Papa God gave them.

Then they turned eighteen, and aliens invaded their brains. Or so it seemed.

We decided that the hardest part of mothering is when our sweet little babies grow up and begin to make their own choices. That, dear sister, is when we become tree stumps. You know, like in Shel Silverstein's classic book, *The Giving Tree* (which, ironically, most of us read to our little ones). In the allegory, the tree (mother) has given all she has to the boy throughout his entire life—her time for companionship, her fruit for nourishment, her shade for protection, her limbs for shelter, until all that's left of her is the stump. But she doesn't stop there. She offers him her stump to rest on when he's old, after he has taken the best of her without even realizing it (or really appreciating it), and she has willingly given her all.

But she's still willing to give more. Just like you. Just like me.

We're stumps, girls. Regardless of what pathetic little is left of us, we offer it to our children because:

❀ We conceived them and brought them into this world.

❀ We nurtured them through good and bad, rejoicing and heartbreak.

❀ We bound up their wounds and kissed their boo-boos.

❀ We love them for who they are—a piece of our own heart—not for what they do or don't do.

❀ Inseparably wrapped up in them is our hope for the future.

And those are the same reasons your heavenly Papa loves you. Beyond your confusion and heartbreak. Beyond this day and even this life. Beyond every doubt.

God is closest to those with broken hearts.

~JEWISH PROVERB

FOLLOWING MY PERSONAL GPS (GOD-POWERED SATELLITE)

1. Going back to the first page in this chapter, in your life, what's the palm tree to your oak? Has someone or something—it may be reality or even a longtime fervent dream—been ripped away from your loving embrace, leaving you with your arms surrounding emptiness?

2. How are you dealing with that heartbreak?

3. Are there any unresolved hidden hurts in your heart? Have you had a Lt. Dan episode when you duked it out with God?

4. Do you ever cope with heartbreak by turning off your emotions? When? How did that work for you?

5. Is there a prodigal whose spiritual eyes you can pray to be opened by Papa God's extensive kindness, tolerance, and patience as found in Romans 2:4 (on page 205)?

CHAPTER 23

Can You Feel the Love? Or at Least the Like?
(Loving-Kindness)

*Make every effort to add to your faith. . .
mutual affection; and to mutual affection, love.*
2 PETER 1:5–7 NIV

I'm mesmerized by the grainy black-and-white photo of a tiny woman resting against a mountain boulder, her wispy white hair pulled back from her wrinkled face and tucked beneath a weathered black hat. Kindness radiates from her eyes. She grips a crooked wooden cane with her right hand; calluses, age spots, and gnarled fingers bear testimony to an incredible hundred-year life of service to others.

If you didn't know better, you might think she appears frail, but appearances can be deceiving. This is one of the strongest women who ever graced the earth.

She wears a white apron over her dark, long-sleeved, ankle-length cotton dress. If you look closely, you'd swear you can see the nails she hammered into the soles of her worn leather ankle boots for traction in the ice and snow during her routine treks over rugged Blue Ridge mountain terrain to deliver over one thousand babies between 1890 and 1939.

Her name is Orelena Hawks Puckett, and her life of giving was borne of pain.[16]

Married at sixteen, Orelena gave birth to twenty-four babies—
two dozen babies—none of which lived past infancy. Not one lived
long enough to toddle around Orelena's crude plank mountain
cabin, wear the little sweaters she lovingly sewed by hand, ride on
her husband's wide shoulders, or sit at Orelena's knee by the fire-
place and listen to stories by candlelight. Not one.

Now I know many of you reading this have struggled with the
anguish of infertility. Some have lost your precious, eagerly awaited
baby far too soon after you first held him or her in your arms.
Some have made the agonizing decision of allowing someone else
to raise your child. Others, like me, have suffered miscarriages and
never got to see that tiny slice of your heart before angels whisked
him or her away to Jesus' cradle.

But to lose twenty-four babies?

Can you imagine the heartache? The devastation of burying
yet another sweet child you'd held to your breast, sung to, prayed
over, and dreamed of a promising future for?

After the heart-wrenching death of so many dreams, you'd
think the utter disappointment would result in relentless depression for any woman. But not Orelena Puckett. The Lord provided
a way to heal her shattered heart by helping other women receive
the blessing she had yearned for. Orelena began delivering babies
at a time and location where a chronic shortage of doctors often
resulted in the loss of both mother and baby during childbirth.

Orelena dedicated her life to learning all she could to become
a skilled midwife. Expectant parents throughout the vast, rugged
Appalachians sought her out because of her compassion and kindness, which were legendary. Orelena never said no, regardless of
how many miles she had to travel on foot or horseback, night or
day, sleet or snow, driving rain or blistering heat. Her commitment
to help others no matter her personal cost resulted in the successful

delivery of over one thousand babies, the last of which—her own great-great-grandnephew—she delivered the same year she died at age 102.

One thousand lives. . .lives that might very well have been lost without Orelena giving, giving, and giving even more. Such is the amazing legacy of loving-kindness one tiny mountain woman left behind.

That's the kind of legacy I want to be remembered for—don't you?

DO IT FOR LOVE

Loving-kindness is one of my all-time favorite phrases, but sadly it's not one we hear much these days. Used over twenty-five times in the Old Testament alone (KJV), it perfectly describes Papa God's giving nature toward His beloved children. Loving-kindness combines the tenderness and affection of agape, phila, and storge love all rolled into one. A single word that conveys the profound motivational force behind selfless giving.

You know, giving and kindness are soul sisters—the offspring of sacrificial love.

You'll rarely find one sister without the other. They work in tandem like two hands. Giving is the calloused hand of tireless work on someone else's behalf. Kindness often wears a velvet glove. But they both respond as strong, capable fingers reaching out to offer help when help is most needed. Neither draws attention to itself; neither is brassy or brash or boastful.

In fact, both are extraordinarily silent. Like snow softly falling to coat and smooth the rough, jagged edges of this world with pure, pristine loveliness.

But despite its ethereal beauty, giving often hurts. It's not a pleasant process to relinquish something we highly value, even when we know it will be used and enjoyed by someone else. That's why it's called sacrificial. Giving is truly a sacrifice—something we willingly give up, although we'd really rather not.

Corrie ten Boom, a Christian Dutch woman who sacrificially gave everything she had to hide Jews from the Nazis in World War II, said, "Hold everything in your hands lightly, otherwise it hurts when God pries your fingers open."

We weren't meant to clutch our possessions with an iron grip. They, like this life, are only temporary and will soon pass away. Why not share them to make some else's existence a little better?

I will never forget the illustration of selfless giving related by Pam Cope in her wonderful book, *Jantsen's Gift*. Pam, whose fifteen-year-old son Jantsen died suddenly and unexpectedly in 1999, redirected her grief into establishing the Touch a Life Foundation, a nonprofit organization that builds shelters for homeless children in Vietnam and children rescued from slavery in Northern Ghana.[17]

The story Pam tells about a little orphan girl at the Village of Hope in Northern Ghana sank deep into my heart. The eight-year-old girl, who had very few belongings to call her own, received stickers in the mail from an American couple. She was ecstatic as she jumped up and down, clapping and running about to show everyone her wonderful gift. She then asked for paper to send the couple a thank-you letter and proceeded to joyfully plaster every single sticker she had received on the paper as her way of showing gratitude to the giver for the gift.

In the joy of selfless giving, she gave away her entire gift.

In Pam's wise words, "Maybe the answer to grief, or to feeling lost, is to do what she did: to give recklessly and passionately. . . I believe that in those acts of giving— when you have given away your very last sticker—you become open to receiving life's most tremendous blessings."[18]

OPEN-END DIVIDEND

Giving is a double blessing—to the receiver, of course, but exponentially more so to the giver. "It is more blessed to give than to receive" (Acts 20:35 NKJV). And as a bonus, the unmitigated joy of acting as Papa God's representative in meeting the needs of someone echoes on and on. It never fades away.

I call that concept Open-End Dividend.

All women who have sacrificed for their families understand this truth all too well. When all's said and done, we—the givers— are the ones who are richer for having given. The spiritual benefit is infinite. . .immeasurable. . .open-ended. The gift might be an actual physical item, our severely limited time, or perhaps a spiritual legacy we pass on. . .like trust in Papa God in the face of hardship. But whatever the gift we sacrificially give, we're the ones who feel incredibly blessed.

A Chinese fortune cookie proverb I once opened said, "A bit of fragrance always clings to the hand that gives roses." Ah, I like that.

So what does your hand smell like, sister?

Kindness is something everyone can do. It requires no special knowledge, spiritual gifting, or extra faith. We sometimes just get too busy and bogged down with responsibilities, deadlines, and scrounging up hot dog buns to remember to make kindness a priority. Even at home. *Especially* at home.

I can't count the times I've snapped at one of the peeps I love more than anyone in the world when they've done nothing to deserve it. (Eye roll confession here.) It was me, all me. I suspect you can relate; seems to be a trait common to stressed-out womankind.

Extending kindness to our loved ones is often more difficult than being kind to perfect strangers. Nice, thoughtful strangers who didn't just track mud onto your freshly mopped floor.

I think the apostle Paul's words to his little brother in the faith, Timothy, in the Reach Out translation wraps it up best: "Kindness should begin at home" (1 Timothy 5:4).

Regardless of our excuses—burnt dinner, time crunches, losing battles with the garbage disposal—kindness should begin at home. Because we're teaching by example the importance of biblical loving-kindness to young, ever-observant eyes. Yikes! I think I need that verse on a plaque for my kitchen.

And my bedroom.

And my car.

IT'S A BEAUTIFUL DAY IN THE NEIGHBORHOOD

Okay, girls, our job is pretty clear: "Love your neighbor as yourself" (Galatians 5:14 NLT). So who is our neighbor? Simple: everyone outside our own skin.

Christ-followers don't wait for someone to be kind to us; we show them how it's done. We make it our business to be kind whenever possible. And you know what? As much as we hate to admit it, it's always possible. Kindness is similar to forgiveness in that we don't necessarily have to like the person to be kind to him or her; love and like are oil and water. Sometimes they mix. Sometimes they don't.

That's rather freeing, isn't it? Makes being kind quite doable. Samuel Johnson said, "Kindness is in our power, even when fondness is not."

We might offer our "neighbors" large-scale kindness like Orelena Puckett did. Or kindness on a one-to-one level like the modern-day Good Samaritan who plucked twenty-five-year-old unconscious David (my friend's brother) off the roadside after a truck mirror struck the back of his head while he was riding his bike and sent him sprawling. This total stranger took David to the hospital, stayed with him, and even paid his bills. David had no insurance.

Loving-kindness might play out in small-scale, everyday acts like wheeling your elderly neighbor's garbage can to the curb. Or speaking to Junior in a soft, controlled voice with "sweetie" tacked on the end when he forgets to empty his jeans pocket and you find laundered frog guts in the lint catcher. Or offering a patient smile instead of an angry snarl to the store clerk who shortchanges you.

Snippets of kindness go a long way, you know. I once thought a grumpy, overworked grocery store checkout lady was going to bite my head off and swallow it whole until I racked my brain for something kind to say to her. (Sometimes you have to dig deep.) My simple "You're probably the most efficient bag packer I've ever seen" (which was true!) produced a blush, a grateful smile, and an improved herspective for a brand-new friend.

Loving-kindness might even mean giving away your last sticker. Joyfully!

Kindness is the language which the deaf can hear and the blind can see.
~MARK TWAIN

FOLLOWING MY PERSONAL GPS (GOD-POWERED SATELLITE)

1. Is there something in Orelena Puckett's story that really speaks to you?

2. How about the little African girl who gave away her entire gift to show her gratitude to the giver? Is there a potential gift in your life that you've been holding tightly to? Maybe a little too tightly?

3. Can you recall a time when you were the recipient of Open-End Dividend? When giving hurt but was worth it because you ended up feeling incredibly blessed?

4. Do you find it sometimes more difficult to speak words of loving-kindness at home than to others outside family? Why do you think that is?

5. Is there someone you don't particularly like that you can still be kind to? A nosy Gladys Kravitz clone neighbor, perhaps, or an annoying relative? Hey, why not borrow a page from Orelena and consider delivering their next baby? (Kidding!)

CHAPTER 24

The Future Begins Today
(Hope)

*Absolutely nothing can get between us
and God's love because of the way that
Jesus our Master has embraced us.*

ROMANS 8:39 MSG

‖‖

Do you ever have soggy tea bag days? You know, those times when you feel like a used-up, sapped-out tea bag—worthless, unappreciated, insignificant? I certainly do. Those are the days when the lighthearted buoyancy of love seems a million miles away and six feet under.

It's on soggy tea bag days that it's most important for us to remember that regardless of how we feel (or look) at the moment, we are Papa's poem. That's right, our heavenly Father's poem, His masterpiece, the work of art He created with pen strokes of pure love.

"We are God's masterpiece" (Ephesians 2:10 NLT). The word *masterpiece* here is actually the Greek word *poiema*, from which we derive our English word *poem*.

How 'bout that? Just when we think we're the title character in Mary Shelley's *Frankenstein*, we're actually a beautiful, romantic poem by her husband, renowned poet Percy Shelley. And the best thing about poems is that no two are alike; they are each exquisite and creatively unique in their own way.

Or maybe I should say you-nique. Like you. Like me.

I've never really thought of myself as a poem. Well, maybe something by Dr. Seuss, but little more. Especially on those days when I pretty much look and feel like, well, like a sodden tea bag—frumpy, lumpy, and worthless. Good for nothing except the trash can.

But you know what? I was surprised to learn that used tea bags aren't worthless at all. There are actually dozens of productive uses for them, like taking the sting out of sunburn; soothing tired, puffy eyes; turning gray hair dark again (you can bet I'm going to try this one); stopping foot odor; giving mirrors a streak-free shine; feeding rose bushes; and perking up ferns with a new lush, luxurious demeanor.[19]

Man, I could sure use a new lush, luxurious demeanor myself. A radical makeover. A fresh start.

How about you?

LIVING IN FOREVER LOVE

My writer friend Gil once needed a fresh start after enduring the consequences of a series of bad choices. I admire his six-word memoir (a very cool exercise writers do to develop concise expression; I highly recommend that you give it a try whether you aspire to be a writer or not). Gil's memoir reflects his entire life consolidated into only six words: Lived. Failed. Learned. Reborn. Started over.

Wow. Is that testimony powerful or what?

Renovatio.

Through Christ's sacrificial love for us, a fresh start is not only possible, but it's right there within reach. As refreshing as a rain shower in the desert. As revitalizing as cradling hope in your hands. As restoring as the certainty of living in forever love. And for today, this very moment, as strengthening as living *inside* love . . .enveloped snugly inside Papa God's warm and tender devotion.

Adds an exciting new herspective to being in love, doesn't it?

For once we fall in love—into Papa's love—we can never fall back out of it. It's secure. Safe. Forever. We can't do anything so vile that we lose it. We can't forget about it so long that it fades away. It'll never rust, corrode, or mildew. No one can break it, ruin it, or rip it away from us.

> *And I am convinced that nothing can ever separate us from God's love. Neither death nor life, neither angels nor demons, neither our fears for today nor our worries about tomorrow—not even the powers of hell can separate us from God's love. No power in the sky above or in the earth below—indeed, nothing in all creation will ever be able to separate us from the love of God that is revealed in Christ Jesus our Lord.*
>
> (Romans 8:38–39 NLT)

The truth is that Papa God loves you from the bottom of His heart. And His heart is bottomless.

Isn't that the most liberating feeling? Accepting Papa's unconditional love not only crumbles relationship walls between us and our Savior, but it also frees us from fear of judgment. Hell hath no power over a woman forgiven!

So the takeaway from this book is simple: Papa God's love is never too lost or too late. His love births hope. And without hope, life is meaningless. Yep, you can count on that—without hope, life will soon be meaning less and less.

But with Papa's love shining on you and through you, the future is bright! As His unquenchable love pours into you and overflows from your heart, you can find the power to intentionally love others and live with renewed purpose.

Even if—no, *especially* if—you're a charter member of the sisterhood of recycled tea bags.

> *Hope is that thing with feathers that perches in the soul*
> *and sings the tune without words and never stops. . . .*
>
> ~EMILY DICKINSON

FOLLOWING MY PERSONAL GPS (GOD-POWERED SATELLITE)

1. When was your last soggy tea bag day? Did your tea bag end up being trashed or recycled? How can you improve upon that outcome next time?

2. Okay, tea bag girlfriend, steep on this awhile: What kind of poem do you think Papa God had in mind when He created you? (And don't say "Roses are red, violets are blue, bedbugs are crazy, and so are you!")

3. As a woman, you no doubt have experienced the pain of unrequited love sometime during your life. What reassures you that Papa God's love will always be returned?

4. First John 3:1 (NIV) reminds us, "See what great love the Father has lavished on us, that we should be called children of God." That's *lavish*, as in supersaturate, heap upon, deluge to the point of overflowing. Can you think of at least three ways the Father has lavished love on you?

5. My closing scripture prayer for you, dear sister: "Keep yourselves in God's love as you wait for the mercy of our Lord Jesus Christ to bring you to eternal life" (Jude 1:21 NIV). Amen.

Notes

[1] JOHN 1:12–13 NIV: "To all who did receive him, to those who believed in his name, he gave the right to become children of God."

[2] ROMANS 8:15 NLT: "So you have not received a spirit that makes you fearful slaves. Instead, you received God's Spirit when he adopted you as his own children. Now we call him, 'Abba, Father.' "

[3] 1 JOHN 3:1 NIV: "See what great love the Father has lavished on us, that we should be called children of God!"

[4] "Hell Roads—Tail of the Dragon" www.youtube.com/watch?v=K16YnmJNOfc.

[5] Linda Kline, "Soul Care: Cultivating a Well-Tended Soul," *Just Between Us*, Winter 2013, 14.

[6] "Zucchini Used to Drive Off Bear," *Tampa Tribune*, September 24, 2010.

[7] "Some Crooks So Dumb that it's Just a Crime," *Tampa Tribune*, December 31, 2010.

[8] Ibid.

[9] "Police Free Woman from Pig Swarm," *Tampa Tribune*, August 6, 2011.

[10] "New iPhone, iPad App Keeps Track of Sins," *Tampa Tribune*, February 10, 2011.

[11] "Aha Moments: Five Revelations that Will Change your Marriage," Gary Campbell, PhD, *Homelife*, May 2013, 34.

[12] "50 Famous People with Depression, Mental Illness," Boston's News Channel, www.wcvb.com.

[13] "Depression," Brain & Behavior Research Foundation, www.bbrfoundation.org.

[14] "Surgeon Harvests Pea Sprout from Patient's Lung," *Tampa Tribune*, August 13, 2010.

[15] "Stranger's Kindness Repaid by a Fellow Driver," *Tampa Tribune*, November 9, 2011.

[16] The Puckett Institute, www.puckett.org.

[17] Touch a Life Foundation, www.touchalifekids.org.

[18] Pam Cope, *Jantsen's Gift: A True Story of Grief, Rescue, and Grace* (New York: Grand Central Publishing, 2009).

[19] "22 Ways to Use Tea for Beauty, Home, and Garden," Reader's Digest online, http://www.rd.com/home/22-ways-to-use-tea-for-beauty-home-and-garden/.

Visit with the Author

Deb would love to chat with you and even share a few nuggets of truth gift-wrapped in humor with your church or women's group. Check out her "speaking" drop box at www.DeboraCoty. com for more information, and while you're there, click on the icons to connect with Deb on Facebook, Twitter, and through her personal blog, "Living Life in the Crazy Lane" and her blog for aspiring writers, "Grit for the Oyster."

Look for These Other Faith-Inspiring Books
by Debora M. Coty

Fear, Faith, and a Fistful of Chocolate:
Wit and Wisdom for Sidestepping Life's Worries

Do you find yourself hocking up anxiety over and over like a Guernsey regurgitating her cud? Do the what-ifs suck joy out of your very soul? Welcome to the sisterhood of weary worrywarts. But hey, who wants to be a wart? Together we'll explore the reasons fear can keep us imprisoned and learn how to pick the lock.

More Beauty, Less Beast:
Transforming Your Inner Ogre

Whether you're jaded by emotional wounds, unrealistic standards, or lack of confidence, these LOL girlfriend-to-girlfriend tips will help you transform your destructive inner beast into the exquisite beauty you were always meant to be. When Papa God measures a woman, the tape doesn't go around her hips; it goes around her heart.

Too Blessed to Be Stressed:
Inspiration for Climbing Out of Life's Stress-Pool

If you're searching for peace for your frazzled heart, hope for a better tomorrow, and a smile for your stress-creased face, you'll cherish these uplifting biblically based insights for revitalization of spirit, body, and faith. Sometimes every woman needs a life preserver in the churning everyday stress-pool.

Too Blessed to Be Stressed Perpetual Calendar

A delightful little spiral, flip-style, standing calendar that provides chuckles and inspiration excerpted from *Too Blessed to Be Stressed* for each day of the year. Makes a terrific gift!

Too Blessed to Be Stressed 2015 Planner

A lovely purse-sized daily planner designed to help organize your day through complete month displays plus plenty of room for daily notes. Enjoy scripture and hilarious quips from *Too Blessed to Be Stressed* for more blessings than stressings throughout 2015.

The Bible Promise Book: Too Blessed to Be Stressed Edition

Scads of Bible promises about faith, gratitude, laughter, mercy, peace, trust, relationships, and more. Each scripture will draw you ever closer to your heavenly Father. The Bible is full of promises; when Papa God makes a promise, you can trust it.

Too Blessed to Be Stressed Journal

This stylish, hardcover journal includes the complete text of Debora's popular book *Too Blessed to Be Stressed* and will fill your spirit with Papa God's grace through the ups, downs, and in-betweens of life.

About the Author

Debora M. Coty is a popular speaker, humorist, columnist, longtime Bible student, and award-winning author of numerous books and magazine and newspaper articles. When she's not pecking away at a keyboard, Deb serves in the children's ministry at her church and is an orthopedic occupational therapist (for thirty-five years and counting), writing workshop instructor, and tennis addict. Mother of two married children and one adorable grandbuddy who lives next door, Deb lives and loves in central Florida with her husband, Chuck, and desperately wicked pooch, Fenway.